On Doing Local History

ABOUT THE SERIES
The American Association for State and Local History Book Series publishes technical and professional information for those who practice and support history, and addresses issues critical to the field of state and local history. To submit a proposal or manuscript to the series, please request proposal guidelines from AASLH headquarters: AASLH Editorial Board, 1717 Church St., Nashville, Tennessee 37203. Telephone: (615) 320-3203. Website: www.aaslh.org.

ABOUT THE ORGANIZATION
The American Association for State and Local History (AASLH), a national history organization headquartered in Nashville, TN, provides leadership, service, and support for its members, who preserve and interpret state and local history in order to make the past more meaningful in American society. AASLH is a membership association representing history organizations and the professionals who work in them. AASLH members are leaders in preserving, researching, and interpreting traces of the American past to connect the people, thoughts, and events of yesterday with the creative memories and abiding concerns of people, communities, and our nation today. In addition to sponsorship of this book series, the Association publishes History News, a newsletter, technical leaflets and reports, and other materials; confers prizes and awards in recognition of outstanding achievement in the field; and supports a broad education program and other activities designed to help members work more effectively. To join the organization, go to www.aaslh.org or contact Membership Services, AASLH, 1717 Church St., Nashville, TN 37203.

On Doing Local History

Third Edition

Carol Kammen

ROWMAN & LITTLEFIELD
Lanham • Boulder • New York • Toronto • Plymouth, UK

Published by Rowman & Littlefield
4501 Forbes Boulevard, Suite 200, Lanham, Maryland 20706
www.rowman.com

10 Thornbury Road, Plymouth PL6 7PP, United Kingdom

British Library Cataloguing in Publication Information Available

Library of Congress Cataloging-in-Publication Data
Kammen, Carol, 1937–
On doing local history / Carol Kammen. — Third edition.
pages cm.
ISBN 978-0-7591-2369-4 (cloth) — ISBN 978-0-7591-2370-0 (pbk.) —
ISBN 978-0-7591-2371-7 (electronic) 1. United States—History, Local—Handbooks, manuals, etc. 2. Local history. I. Title.
E180.K28 2014
973—dc23
                                                            2013046453

Michael Kammen
1936–2013
He is a portion of the loveliness
Which once he made more lovely . . .

Contents

Foreword

I have admired Carol Kammen's work for some time. Her column in *History News*, spanning almost twenty years, continues to present a welcome and refreshing view of the historians' craft. Tightly constructed, eminently readable, and always relevant, Kammen's editorials define the genre of local history and establish high standards for its practitioners.

The importance of her sense of the past was reinforced last year when I taught a freshmen-level introductory history course. Titled "Making History," the offering was designed to answer questions such as "What is history?," "What do historians do?," "What is historical evidence?," and "Why is knowledge of history important?"

Over the course of the semester, we explored the nature of history and considered the place of history in our everyday lives. Topics included the construction of historical interpretations, the difference between history and memory, the use of history in manipulating public memory, and the centrality of history in this nation's culture wars. Undergirding the course was an emphasis on local history that allowed the students to take advantage of museums, cemeteries, and past community notables.

My students used three books that covered a wide spectrum of historical inquiry. As I prepared the syllabus, I imagined my students weighing the three offerings somewhat equally and leaving the class with historical nuggets gleaned from the variety of the readings. Only a few weeks into the semester, however, it became very clear that my students fully embraced only one of the texts and that was *On Doing Local History*! They were captivated not only by the manner in which Kammen made local history interesting (the concept of local history being something quite foreign to those recent high school graduates), but also the style with which she presented her information. *On Doing Local History* provided them a logically constructed window through which they could view and understand the nature of history. Because Kammen has such an obvious gift for conceptualizing and writing about local history, my students departed my class with a much greater appreciation for the idea of history and how history is constructed and used, locally and nationally.

This third edition of *On Doing Local History* contains all of the informative essays of the previous versions. Readers will additionally benefit from a new compelling chapter on doing ecclesiastical history and an inspired meditation on the public benefits of encouraging Clio to interact with other muses of the arts and humanities. She proposes here that if an understanding of history is enhanced by the inclusion of art and music, then clearly the public presentation of music and art can be enriched when accompanied by historical context. Our sense of history— local, public, and general—is equally enhanced by the intelligent analysis of Clio's profession found in *On Doing Local History*.

Having a high regard for Kammen's ability to craft clear and powerful sentences, I turned to that old standby *The Elements of Style* to find adjectives to better describe her work. I was reminded that like Kammen, William Strunk and E. B. White were both associated with Cornell University: Strunk as a professor and White as a student. I do not know whether Kammen is a follower of Strunk and White, but she clearly shares their gift for effective writing. There must be something literary in the air "high above Cayuga's waters."

Dwight T. Pitcaithley
New Mexico State University

Introduction

Some years ago, when I was quite young, I was searching for a way to be useful within the limits of my own skills and life. I had studied history and lived among historians, so looking at local and regional history seemed possible and was interesting to me. Finding a niche within which to do this was actually more difficult than deciding what I would like to do. There was no role for me in the local historical society, run by old-timers in the community, all more than fifty years older than I, and perhaps wiser, I don't know. They had their way of doing things and thought my interest a passing fancy since I was not born locally. I would surely, they thought, move on to other, more lucrative activities—or simply move on.

I didn't, however, move. Instead, I worked my way though the local archives, read through the old newspapers, and began thinking about some of the larger aspects of local history. I read local histories and history journals and at one point wrote a highly agitated letter to Jerry George, then-editor of *History News*, complaining about all the topics not touched on in that journal. It was, I remember writing, too organizational, so overly concerned with creating a professional presence it neglected what was the core, that of doing of local history.

Writing letters of agitation is a good way of disposing of an issue; concern attended to, one can move on. And we did, going to Paris to live for a year. But my concerns about local history and the way it was approached lingered and were caught up by a letter from Jerry and his colleagues inviting me to write about local history.

So in our little flat on the Rue du Pointoise, with the Seine less than a block away, I began writing about local history. I read from the American Library and thought a good deal. At the end of the year I returned with manuscript pages—something that would never happen today with our puters and devices—of nine chapters about local history. That resulted in the first edition of *On Doing Local History.*

I attempted in that book to expand beyond the standard "how to write about local history" to something that discussed why we do what we do, sources, what our choices mean, how we influence what we say, how the times matter, and what local history means to the community. I urged people who are concerned with local history to consider a variety of sources, leave footnotes of the sort that they wish others had left for them, think about their own community or subject in a regional or national context, and see how their own abilities and interests—and the time in which they wrote—determined the questions that they asked and sought to answer. I was far less interested in describing what a proper note card might contain—or its shape and size—than in urging that a range of documents would expand what they had to say, and that asking questions of what had been said in the past was important.

I was writing during what I have come to see as a significant swelling of interest in local history, those two dozen or so years following the Bicentennial of the American Revolution, when even some academic historians were looking at local records in order to answer questions about our national past. It was a time, also, when some communities were reprinting older histories; some individuals were writing new ones based on older histories but in general following those older patterns.

It was an era, too, when a new sort of historian appeared on the home front. Programs in public history began in the late 1970s and these well-trained individuals were spreading out over the land. They made a difference in smaller historical societies, bringing their interest in context, in race, gender, and sometimes class. They also often saw beyond the historical society door. Their biggest difference, however, was that they came into a community in which they had not lived, and in which they might not remain. They broke the pattern of who was involved with local history and broadened its outlook and its methods. Their appearance also changed historical societies in that they were often the first paid employees, requiring a refocusing of a board's activities from arranging speakers for an annual meeting to finding funds for salaries. They professionalized local history and influenced even history organizations too small or too localized to even consider paid employees.

It was for this changing world of local history that I wrote. For those who wanted to write about their hometowns, as people have done for several centuries, for those involved with the collecting of local documents and artifacts, for those in local history organizations, and those who were community history boosters. I hoped that my book would help all these folks: the traditionalists and the newcomers, the well rooted and those bare-root people who moved from place to place who might find local history a way to "enter" a community. Or, at least to understand where they were in time and place—and to see how they got there. I was interested in the large figure in the carpet and in the border, in the unique and in what was a regional pattern.

I thought at the time I wrote *On Doing* that I had a bunch of the answers for all these folks. I was very pleased, on a visit to Utah, when the graduate students at Brigham Young University called *On Doing* "the local history bible."

I wrote a history of my county, another of my city, a history of the university at which I taught, and about African Americans at the university achieving higher education; I edited a couple of books, and in 1995 I began writing the editorials for *History News*—something that has been an honor and a great pleasure. I have worked with a number of editors of that journal and have learned from them, and have heard from a great number of readers—some of whom told me that I didn't know everything, and a few who thought I didn't know much. And I appreciated each and every comment—though the positive ones were much nicer to dwell on than the others—and all of them have given me a lot to think about.

Today, I would write *On Doing* somewhat differently than I first did. I find I am less strident today than in the past; I know less now than I thought I did; I am more tolerant of some practices that I once would have condemned because I have used some of them myself. I think I am more generous today. At least I hope so.

For this edition of *On Doing Local History* I have read through the manuscript; I have tried to make my statements clearer and perhaps even more elegant. I have taken out some statements that bothered me, I have updated references, and I have added a good deal of new material. I have included two new essays that I think expand what I have tried to preach and perhaps explain in a somewhat different way what we might ideally do. One is titled "Clio and Her Sisters," about history's cooperation with the other arts; the other is boldly titled, "How to Write a Congregational History," about just that: some of the ways we might approach a common local history topic. Each essay was a commission and each appears here with permission.

What I realize, more than ever, is that 2014 is a very different time than the 1980s when this book was first written. Some of the topics that then seemed new and perhaps a bit daunting are standard today, such as discussions about ethnicity, or race, or community problems. These were touched on some years ago but today are standard fare. The concerns of historical organizations today are also different. The 1980s was a time of organizational building—sometimes wisely and sometimes not—but many historical groups were formed then and were just starting out. Today many of those same groups are folding, while others are stricken with economic woes, because a crucial concern of all historical organizations today is financial.

The electronic world has changed just about everything, offering great opportunities for history organizations but also some severe challenges. In addition, the field of public history has grown tremendously and its students are everywhere, in museums, state history organizations, in government and companies, in communities. Today books about the doing of history fill shelves in local libraries and archives, for attention *has* been paid to how we think about history, about memory, about our communities, about how we approach historical topics. Today we have sources at our fingertips, bringing distant documents and information to our desktops. It is amazing what continues to appear online.

The writing of local history has also changed with the appearance of Arcadia and other presses that have supported and encouraged publication of books about localities. The list of books that AASLH and Rowman & Littlefield produce is also wide ranging, reflecting new concerns and interests—and challenges. One important book is *Writing Local History Today: A Guide to Researching, Publishing, and Marketing Your Book* by Thomas A. Mason and J. Kent Calder (2013) that deals with many questions that arise when bringing research to the public.

I am very aware that people in our communities have a great array of things that demand their attention today. Local history does not exist in a vacuum but as in a shopping mall where there are many desirable choices. It is up to us to see that what we display will entice, and educate.

For many years, I have written from Ithaca, New York, and about the area and in doing so I have learned a great deal. I still have passion about the history of my locality and the doing of local history, along with concerns about how we think about local history, about context and complexity, about the growth of community and the perpetuation of memory—and of myth. Old and new commingle on these pages and it thrills me to know that local history has grown, has faced new topics, and has reacted to new opportunities. This book is written with the idea that I am involved and so are you the reader, and that together we can bring to our communities, in a variety of forms, interest, education, and enlightenment about the local past. We do so because we are interested, because we care, because we want our communities to know their history—and because we know that it is important.

Carol Kammen

Chapter One

Local History's Past

Local history is not only a challenge to the most highly trained master of historical techniques; it is also—and long may it remain!—the last refuge of the non-specialist.
—H. P. R. Finberg, "Local History" (1962)[1]

Local history is the memory of place. It is most often crafted by someone who lives in the locality, often someone untrained in historical method but who has an idea of what needs to be remembered, what should be celebrated, what it is that is important for residents to know. Many people come to local history following in a family tradition of interest, or because they hold a position that leads them to want to codify what is known, or to understand about the ground on which they live. Interest probably comes first before method or system. Sometimes reverence for place or a sense of awe of the past drives the local historian; sometimes it is a desire to know what happened. The local historian has always been curious, has always asked questions, has collected information and has found ways of communicating it—in the past, mostly by writing down the story of his or her home place. There has never been one way to "do" local history and it has generally been conducted uniquely, although not without motive. Often that motive has been to answer a question, sometimes the motive was to enshrine a segment of the past; very often the motive of the local historian has been to transmit a message to the present.

Local history is sometimes clouded in myth, colored by forms of ancestor worship, or confused with ideas of patriotism or boosterism. It can be dated to the sixteenth century in England, especially to the frequently cited book by William Lambarde, *The Perambulation of Kent* (1656), and to approximately the same period in France. Originally, in both countries, local history grew out of an interest in nobility, castles, coinage, parishes, armorial bearings,

1

and lineages. Some of the books produced were well done, if limited in outlook, whereas others were "mere vestiges of error, and some of fraud, which time and vanity had rendered sacred."[2] Most early local histories were written without plan, and whatever information was known about an area was included, sometimes in a haphazard fashion, often in a chronological sequence, and mostly whatever was distasteful or not of interest to the writer, or to the writer's aims and objectives, was ignored. At a time of rather general illiteracy, the local historian had a pen and the means and time to record in whatever fashion suited his (and it was usually, in those early times, a male) purpose. The one thing for sure then, and even today, is that local history was rarely undertaken in order to achieve financial gain—for few local historians have ever made much money from their efforts. Sometimes, however, the local historian gained a sort of immortality, even if in a limited geographical setting.

The pattern of writing history in the New World was little different from that in the Old. Writing history during America's colonial period was often stimulated by political motives, while some history was providential, "proving" God's will and America's unique mission. In the eighteenth century, history writing in the colonies tended to be colored by political views. Books stressed a provincial identity, often with an eye to encouraging immigration.

After the American War of Independence, history tended to justify the actions of Americans, and it attempted to create a national myth to bring disparate colonies and peoples together—to make of many, one nation. Although there were local histories in many settled places, most attempts at writing the history of a particular community date from the 1840s for a good part of the nation. Hermann E. Ludewig, writing in 1846, noted: "No people in the world can have so great an interest in the history of their country, as that of the U.S. of North America: for there are none who enjoy an equally great share in their country's historical acts." He insisted that the history of the United States contains the "political and moral history of mankind, and it points to the way of greater perfection, which a free nation ought continually to strive to attain." Ludewig and others saw the United States as an exceptional nation, a beacon to the world, and the histories of American places a fitting way to commemorate the achievement of community-building. This view gave little consideration to those who were already on the land but celebrated those who came along to build and sustain particular towns and cities.[3]

By and large, writers of local histories prior to 1870 have been called by one scholar "patrician historians."[4] Although "patrician" might aptly describe some, many others among our nineteenth-century authors might better be called members of the nascent professional class whose occupations allowed them the leisure to engage in the writing of history. What these men— and they were nearly all men—had in common was some measure of education that stressed classical literature and an interest in writing essays about their hometowns, which often meant celebrating their own families and those considered original settlers. The newspaper publishers, editors, lawyers, doctors, and ministers who wrote much of the earliest nineteenth-century local history had some common concerns, and because they generally created the first—and sometimes the only—history of a community, their attitudes toward history writing influenced the writing of local history thereafter. Their style of writing and the topics they addressed shaped the public's idea of what local history was and how it should be presented. They created the patterns from which many local historians have only over the past fifty years freed themselves.

These early writers hoped to lure settlers to their communities. They promoted the healthy situation of their towns or counties, discounting reports of persistent problems such as bad water, isolation, illness, or lack of opportunity. Many of their histories were commemorative—a memorial to or a remembrance of the early settlers. H. C. Goodwin, in 1859, wrote that writing a local history "is a duty which we of the present generation owe to the memory of the pioneers of civilization in the region of the country where we dwell, to gather up with care whatever records of the times there are left, and studying them well, transmit them in the most enduring form to successive ages."[5] And if Goodwin wrote because of a duty the present owed to the past, then Franklin B. Hough wrote because "there are certain duties which the Present owes to the Future, to transmit in a permanent form the record of the Past, that the memory of olden time, and the names of those who have aided in the formation of society fall not into oblivion."[6] There was little room, in this optimistic view, for the Native American, or for those who did not succeed, or for others not designated as town-builders.

Some local histories were written to show the degree of culture to be found in an area, so that a community would not be written off as backward or regarded by its residents (or others) as a backwater. To this end, a number of authors produced promotional pamphlets in the guise of history. "The contrast," wrote one author in 1847, extolling the present state of his village as compared with its rude beginnings some fifty years earlier,

> is hardly to be comprehended. The change from toil, privation, and constant efforts to those of ease, repose, and tranquility; from the hardy pioneer's life, to one of affluence and splendor; from the rustic garb to the finer and most costly fabrics of American and English manufacture; from a dense wilderness, to rich, fertile fields; from low, filthy, and miasmatic lagoons, to dry, healthy, and beautiful flower gardens; from the absence of learning and literary pursuit, to the flooding of every species of intelligence.[7]

Progress was regarded, in this case, as that which improved life and eased toil: the word "civilization" was often used to denote culture rather than rudeness or primitive conditions, or even what some thought of as savagery. Change tended to be viewed as ominous, however, when it brought about alterations in the character of the population or in the mores of a community from that which the earliest settlers aspired to or the local historian extolled. Progress could mean increase: from little to fulfillment, from overlooked to renown, from want to plenty. For those people who worked hard, it was the deserved and expected reward. Other changes were seen as destructive of old values when they created diversity of population or moved leadership from those people who had traditionally held power and influence to newcomers or those perceived to be outsiders.

The Fourth of July was an occasion when history was sometimes expounded in an oral presentation. When public lectures became the vogue in our communities, the history of a town was often considered a fitting topic. These orations frequently treated events as if chronology alone were history, yet the public found such recitations acceptable and even enjoyable, and they tended, when published, to be popular souvenirs.[8] Putting a date on an event was deemed an appropriate historical activity.

Some histories were imitative or a form of competition, written because another community (particularly a neighbor or rival for population, manufacturing, or prestige) already had such a record. "That which suggested the present enterprise and which has resulted in the production of the following history," noted one author in 1840, was the reading of another town's book.[9] He then asserted that his community's history "would not be without interest even to the present generation." This last statement reveals another important motivation for the writing of local history. Local histories were often regarded as inspirational and instructional, especially to the youth of a community—those young people who took for granted and were perhaps even disenchanted with the opportunities to be found in the places where they lived. The unrelenting story in these "small histories" is of a hardy pioneer who moved to virgin land and, by dint of hard work and belief in the Christian religion, made for himself and his family the rosy existence that they presently enjoyed. The hardy pioneer's wife is rarely mentioned, but that is another problem altogether. These histories present a didactic lesson, even to the contemporary generation, and "cannot fail to be deeply interesting and instructive to the present inhabitants." Used extensively in the past, "virgin forest" is a term that today makes us wince because it implies that the land was lying there unused and unpeopled waiting for the arrival of Americans of European descent with their own ideas of how the land should be regarded, divided, and developed.[10]

Some histories, like newspapers of the era, were forms of local boosterism, demonstrating that a small enclave was the center of all that was progressive and enterprising. In fact, these two words, "progress" and "enterprise," recur over and over again in the descriptions of places about which our local historians wrote. They reflected, of course, the very words that the settling generation used: the first steamboat on Cayuga Lake, launched in the early 1820s was called *The Enterprise*. Comparable examples abound.

These histories promoted a town, boosted its image, and attempted to demonstrate—especially to youth—that prosperity could be found at home. They also played on feelings of local pride and clannish associations. "Those who read this volume," stated one historian, "will find their fathers or ancestors, their relations or acquaintance," for the book was about the land of their nativity—or perhaps of their adoption, in which case their good sense was taken as approval of place and an indication of sensible choice. Such sentiments were important to cultivate, the same writer noted, "because it is upon the love of family and country, that all the social and virtuous affections are based." Ultimately, these histories represent a form of filiopietism, or local ancestor worship, of patriotism and attachment to the particular place where one belonged.[11]

George Callcott, writing in 1970, claimed that the pre–Civil War interest in local history "has never since been equaled." This, however, ignores the fact that the boom in local history really came after that war, when in 1876 President Ulysses S. Grant called on Americans to write the histories of their hometowns. Nor, writing in 1970, could Callcott know what was about to occur in the next three decades, for there was an interesting and important post-1976 blossoming. Callcott observed of those nineteenth-century histories that "the more geographically limited the interests of historians were, the more modest their accomplishments" and that town histories were written by a lot of "generally poor historians." This might be true when judging early local histories by the standards of academic history today, yet they are valuable today for what these authors recorded if not for their research methods and narrative. Those histories with a broader geographic base, he claimed, tended to have a more lasting impact; for example, Timothy Flint and John Wesley Monette's histories of the Mississippi Valley or Henry Howe's historical collections of the West were more important to Callcott than town chronicles that were "generally detailed, highly factual, liberally sprinkled with genealogy, and frequently 700 pages or more in length."[12] Certainly it is true that a broader region required the historian to see general patterns, to use material to support a larger theme, and to explain rather than to recount. However, discounting the importance to communities of even the more restricted histories should not be done lightly.

Local histories were often written to promote local and national heroes. Indeed, those books usually mention the major figures in a town's past, and certainly every "important figure" who passed through the area is given his due. These histories do more than promote public heroes, though. They tend, over time, to democratize heroism: that is, they imply heroism in Everyman, or at least in every citizen of the community (excluding, of course, African

Americans, transients, women, and people whose position was marginal, such as laborers and tenant farmers and Indians). Each settler mentioned in local history was someone who had selected that place, and each had built a life for himself and his family that embodied outward, or public, satisfaction. Those who did not succeed, or did not remain, were omitted from the history, many because they were not seen as important to the life of the community and others because they lacked the funds to pay the subscription fees required for inclusion. Those men who stayed in a community appeared upstanding, and strove to show their material success, earthly rewards which might foreshadow a Christian afterlife. They appeared in heroic or at least historic proportions—something that had been, in the past, reserved for a few, not available to "almost any man." The success of the early settlers, said one author, "induced many to look with desire" toward his country. Where history in Europe concentrated on the church and the manor, the priest and the lord, local history in the United States extolled the successful businessman, the upstanding farmer. If these sounds rather like Thomas Jefferson's yeoman farmer, the backbone of a republican society, it is no accident. [13]

Jefferson's views were known to most of the writers of our mid-nineteenth-century local histories, but so were the opinions, styles of writing, and literary conventions of classical historians writing of Greece and Rome. Many educated American males—the patrician or leisured historians—knew Latin and Greek or read the ancients in translation; in the examples given in their histories and in the language patterns with which they wrote, we can hear classical authors—and sometimes the King James version of the Bible—echo through our own American setting.

Washington Irving laid out his debt to and knowledge of the classic historical tradition in his *Knickerbocker's History of New York*. He stated that, like Herodotus, who lacked written records, he endeavored to "continue the chain of history by well authenticated traditions"; that, like Xenophon, he maintained the utmost impartiality and the strictest adherence to truth; and that, as in the manner of Sallust, he enriched his history with portraits of "ancient worthies," drawn at full length and faithfully colored. Thucydides had taught him to season his history with political speculations; but, as had Tacitus, Irving sweetened that which he wrote with the "graces of sentiment" and infused the whole with the "dignity, grandeur and magnificence of Livy." Finally, he had, like Polybius, sought to make out of the disparate facts that came to hand a history that had unity. [14] Washington Irving's history of Manhattan is satirical in tone, intended to amuse the public and to sell books. It is a literary tour de force, written pen in cheek. Most other local historians took themselves and their histories rather more seriously, expecting and receiving somewhat less of a monetary return and in general no literary reputation.

Local history became popular in the Centennial era spurred on by President Ulysses S. Grant's call to Americans to write the histories of their localities. The nation was seen as the sum of its parts. Literacy was the norm, and for some people there was increased leisure time and a great interest in self-improvement, one route to which was history, which provided Americans with what might be viewed as a common cultural literacy. All studied and read it.

While the centennial in 1876 contributed to the explosion of interest in the writing of local history, other things, too, spurred interest in the field. The historian John Higham has pointed out that during the nineteenth century "the study of history in various forms . . . superseded the study of the classics as the chief vehicle for enabling man to know himself."[15] This shift from the classics to history can be seen throughout the century. One writer of local history noted that there were two sources of information—philosophy and history. The former addressed itself to understanding, whereas history enhanced understanding and the imagination and wakened the sympathies of the heart. Of the two, history, he wrote, is the more important. Having minimized philosophy, the author looked more closely at history and posed a new dilemma for himself. He recognized the study of antiquity as the greatest subject of history. How then can he reconcile the values of antiquity with the fact that the work he was presenting to the public was one of American local history—a subject barely two generations old? Easily done, purrs our clever author: the antiquity of the world is the story of its creation and of the people of ancient civilizations. So, too, the antiquity of the author's section of America is told as the story of its creation by means of its era of settlement and of the valiant pioneers who struggled to make it home. Although that settlement took place only fifty years earlier, he argues, it still had all the charm "as it would have if it had taken [place] five hundred years ago!"[16]

There are some less attractive reasons, too, why people turned to local history during this period. The last twenty years of the nineteenth century was an era of increased immigration to the United States by people whose ethnic diversity challenged the hegemony of native-born Americans; it was a time when class divisions became apparent and were heightened by industrialization, when political disillusionment, fear of the unruly, and labor unrest swept the nation. Few of these aspects of the times were treated by the local historical societies forming at the time, for those associations became the refuge of people who felt beleaguered by change and who feared that their way of life might not survive the onslaught. Local histories recalled old times; they chronicled the genesis of a community, its first settlers, its prominent citizens, and the values they shared. Local histories presented a history of steady progression from rude beginnings to a contemporary civilized state, with home, family, patriotism, hard work, and Christianity brought along intact "to illustrate the privations, virtues, piety, patriotism, and enterprise of her people," as one history of a New York community states. [17] All the while, the treatment accorded to the pioneers of a community became a sanctified litany, a legacy that remains with us today.

Other motives offered by writers of local histories near the end of the nineteenth century include a desire to "rescue materials from fast-gathering oblivion" and a concern to collect the memories of older persons who were eyewitness to what happened, or recalled the stories of their own pioneer ancestors. Some writers wanted to "correct many errors" in past historical accounts and to "correctly narrate these important historical events." [18]

Gilbert W. Hazeltine's preface to his *The Early History of the Town of Ellicott*, in Chatauqua County, New York, sums up the motivations and style of many of these nineteenth-century gentleman writers. Hazeltine was a local doctor, and his preface, while lengthy, is so exemplary that it deserves our attention. It is unclear who was "to the manor born." This might have been Hazeltine's claim to having created a modest volume or to stake himself as a member of middle class, or a jab at historians in the academy working on larger, more national projects, which would have been deemed of greater importance, hinting at the lower status of local studies.

What is the *ratio justifica* of this book? Simply this. Our friends desired us to write it, and we wrote it; the Journal Printing Company printed it, and Merz put on the covers. It is a homemade book for home use; and the critics, if any, we expect to be to the manor born.

Our friends will justify themselves by saying,—"we desired to rescue the memory of our grandfathers and our grandmothers, and our parents, from the deep pall of oblivion which was fast settling down upon them—and the history of their homes in the wilderness, in which they labored so hard to secure blessings which we alone have lived, to reap and to enjoy. The hardy, generous, and in many instances gifted men and women, who lived and labored in what are now our busy streets, have left enduring monuments of their united labor, but the records of their individual selves, have been meager and unsatisfactory. The records imprinted on the memories of a few yet living—whose boyhood days were spent in Jamestown, before it had become an incorporated village, have been found, of all remaining sources of information, the most reliable and satisfactory. There are still living here a number of persons who became citizens from 1825 to 1835, whose memory of events has yielded material assistance by sustaining and strengthening the memory of the writer,—by what they themselves knew of, and had frequently heard related, of the early settlers. As the years roll on, their deeds would soon have been forgotten, if the extended sketches we have caused to be made by one who was an onlooker, had not been written and given to the world." This is the answer you elicit from our friends.

It has been our attempt to record the names and the deeds of the fathers, surrounded by all that constituted their homes—as we once saw them, and as, to-day, they are vividly depicted in our memory. We have labored to place before you, their children and successors—pictures of their persons,—their homes,—and their surroundings in the long ago when Jamestown was a hamlet in the wilderness—when the Pearl City was the Rapids—when instead of the busy hum of a hundred factories and a thousand industries, and a city of comfortable homes and palace residences there were a few lowly dwellings, and the hum was of the saw mill and the busy boatman by day, and the howl of the wolf or the scream of the wild cat in the Big Fly, by night. The homes, the industries, the scenes here depicted, were to our noble but humble-minded fathers the all of human life—they bounded the horizon of their being—they were the environments of their existence. Memory had embalmed them in the hearts of their children, now few remaining, old and fast passing away. What is known of these Pioneers among the children's children, the present generation, is weak and shadowy, and is yearly becoming more and more dim, and at the end of another decade—even within that short period—folk lore would have claimed the little remaining of the memory of the early settlers. We interpose this feeble book to prevent such a disaster. We present it as a rough monument to their memories—their homes—their deeds—their lives.

Although conscious that we have used every effort, which could be reasonably expected, to accurately describe the scenes and events herein depicted, yet the invariable experience of others should teach us not to claim entire exemption from those errors and imperfections always found in works of biography history. History has been defined [as] "An approximation towards truth: We cannot believe that this definition even approximates to a true one—nevertheless it may embody a shadow of a truth, for every thing human is marked by imperfections."[19]

In the 1880s, history emerged as a profession throughout the United States, and gentleman historians yielded to university professors for whom historical activity was not an avocation but a specialized career. These men made history an institutional product. David Van Tassel ends his book on the origins of the historical profession in the United States with the epitaph that by 1884 "the long age of the amateur historian had ended."[20] Yet, during this era, when departments of history were being instituted in American universities and young men were looking seriously at historical studies as a career, amateur local historians were not daunted—nor did they feel superfluous. At the outset, there was no intention to make a division between the two groups.

Quite the contrary. One of the most influential practitioners of history set out in a very different direction. Herbert Baxter Adams, after having studied for a PhD in Heidelberg, Germany, went to Johns Hopkins University to teach when that institution opened in 1876. Adams had the title of fellow at Johns Hopkins, and he soon began leading a graduate seminar in history. He directed his history students to local topics while he himself prepared a paper on the role that Maryland's delegates had played in the Continental Congress—a paper that he delivered at a meeting of the Maryland Historical Society, which had been created in 1844 in what was the Baltimore City post office building. Adams attempted to promote cooperation between "the local cultural establishment and the emerging professoriat."[21] He stressed the importance of publishing colonial documents, and he urged the state to provide funds so that those materials might be made available to the interested public.

At the same time that Adams was promoting local studies, Charles Kendall Adams, president of Cornell University and a historian, suggested that a professional historical society be formed. Herbert Baxter Adams took the idea forward, and he shepherded the American Historical Association (AHA) into being. It was his intention that the new association include gentleman scholars as well as professionals and that the AHA would provide direction for emerging local historical societies: "The implicit theory of the association was that the professors would lead and yet welcome and honor outstanding amateur historians and seek to coordinate efforts of the many local historical societies."[22]

It did not work out so smoothly, however, for the needs of the professionals and the amateurs did not easily dovetail, nor was one group willing to simply step aside while young men preached the new historical creed. One young professor complained in 1889: "There were more nobs than usual in attendance. . . . I am a little inclined to think the thing is getting into the hands of elderly swells who dabble in history."[23]

The amateurs had their complaints, too. Edward Eggleston wrote that same year that the AHA "seems to be run in the interest of college professors only and to give those of us who are not of that clan the cold shoulder."[24] With some exceptions, the amateurs gradually drifted away. In 1904, they created a Conference of State and Local Historical Societies, meeting in conjunction with the AHA but arranging its own agenda and program.

The amateur historian was certainly eclipsed during these last years of the nineteenth century and in the early days of the twentieth, but by no means did the amateur disappear—a fact ignored in most of the literature concerning the development of historical writing in the United States. Rather, the amateurs persisted, and some continued to write very fine books indeed: Theodore Roosevelt, an accomplished amateur historian, was even made president of the AHA; Franklin D. Roosevelt promoted the history of Hyde Park, New York. Amateurs continued the work of collecting, preserving, and writing local history and of organizing historical organizations. While academic historians tackled national issues, they mostly overlooked the history of America's hometowns.

Throughout the country, local historical societies proliferated and pursued the collecting of documents and artifacts, and local historians produced local studies. Observing the academics, these local historians wished that their work would be more complete and more accurate than previously written local histories and that they could rescue original materials and information otherwise apt to be lost or destroyed. These later local authors submitted themselves to a degree of self-censorship concerning the topics they included in their histories in order—like their predecessors—to present a community's past in its most favorable light. One writer stressed that he wrote only of those events worthy of preservation, while another wanted to create a history "of which all citizens can be proud."[25]

During this era, while other occupations professionalized, the practitioners of local history began to change. Many of the patrician historians—our middle-class gentlemen of some education and local status—removed themselves from the writing of local history, taking up fraternal or social club membership, perhaps, and golf. The newcomers who moved into the field quickly demonstrated that writing local history was a challenge for them and that they were unaccustomed to or at least less than comfortable with the task. Christfield Johnson, who wrote a centennial history of Erie County, New York, noted that his book had taken him fifteen months of continuous work. "Had I known," he complained, "the amount of labor involved, and the very poor pay to be obtained, it is doubtful whether I should have attempted the task." He also wrote: "If any one thinks it easy to harmonize and arrange the immense number of facts and dates here treated of, let him try to learn the precise circumstances regarding a single event, occurring twenty years ago, and he will soon find how widely authorities differ."[26]

Another author stated that his history had taken a quarter of a century to research and write. A third man complained that he had spent fourteen months writing his history. "I have been much puzzled," he wrote, "as to what to leave out. My promise was to make a book of 480 pages," but the completed book required well over eight hundred. Arad Thomas protested that he was "not a professional book maker and has no hope of founding a literary reputation on this work," which he did not do. These complaints had never before been voiced by writers of community histories, some of whom were among America's most luminous literary men, such as Ralph Waldo Emerson, who wrote a history of Concord, Massachusetts. The earlier writers had the education to be comfortable with the task of writing and, with some surety, had picked their way through the tangle of information.[27]

The most significant stimuli to writers of local history at the end of the nineteenth century were the commercial publishers who hired authors, called compilers, to produce local histories. They believed that there was a substantial market for local history, despite the narrow geographical areas involved. These publishers counted on people being willing to pay to have a book containing the names and deeds—and, often, the pictures—of family and friends. The publishers devised a way of meeting their costs before they ever had books to offer for sale, and they thereby faced relatively little financial risk. Throughout the eastern United States there were a number of companies that kept their presses busy by turning out city and county histories. The books offered to the public were fat volumes, full of information and profusely illustrated. These books were not really written but, rather, put together by agents of the publishing company with the aid of people in the community. Nor were these books really narrative history; they were collections of historical sketches, containing a great deal of historical information but little analysis.

If we look at the example of D. Mason and Company, of Syracuse, New York, we can begin to understand the scale of this new undertaking. Mason and Co. published seven New York county histories in seven years while simultaneously being involved with large histories of counties in Ohio and Pennsylvania. In 1884, for example, Mason hired H. P. Smith to compile a history of the City of Buffalo and Erie County. The next year, Smith put together a history of Cortland County, plus a volume on Broome County. Then he moved on. As Smith commented:

> It is the general plan of the publishers in the production of county histories to secure, as far as possible, local assistance in preparing the work, either as writers, or for the purpose of revising all manuscripts; the consequence being that the work bears a local character that could not otherwise be secured, and moreover, comes from the press far more complete and perfect than could possibly be the case were it entrusted entirely to the hands of a comparative stranger to the locality treated of. [28]

Neither Smith nor any of the other compilers who were hired could possibly have written the story of a county in six months. Instead, a compiler would place a notice in a local newspaper to announce his intended project; then he would visit prominent people in the community to solicit their help. He gathered information, invited representatives of industries or individuals and those who knew about local institutions to write blurbs or donate material about themselves for inclusion, and offered them the opportunity to place their pictures in the book. Harold Nestler, who has studied and collected county histories for some time, cites the case of a man who paid W. W. Munsell and Company, an Albany publisher, $150 to have his portrait and biography included in a county history. The subscriber received one copy of the book and twenty extra copies of the photograph. The going rate for such inclusions ranged from $50 to $300 an entry, and in this way the company recovered the cost of the book well ahead of its publication. [29]

Publishers advertised that the biographies included in county histories were representative of men of all professions: that is, that local history was eclectic, not elitist. In these books, we find portraits and biographies of upstanding farmers and businessmen, lawyers, self-made men, and descendants of early pioneer families who had come into the area with little and built comfortable lives for themselves. The common denominator was the ability to pay for inclusion. If each picture included in a county history cost $50, the lowest amount mentioned, then the publishers of an average book, with ninety-six images, could net $4,800 prior to publication. If, on the other hand, the average of the various forms of inclusion, from small portraits to a double-page spread showing house, barn, animals, and inset portraits of other family members, was $100, the publishers could amass, prior to the sales of the book, something in the neighborhood of $9,600. This sum would not cover the cost of publication of a large book today, although it would be an adequate amount of money, even now, with which to begin a project.

Why did people want to be included in such a volume, and at rates that can only be considered steep? What did inclusion in a county history mean to people who paid $100, $150, or more for the privilege? Obviously, one thing these people achieved was a form of immortality. In addition, they established themselves as solid, upstanding citizens, able to buy their way into such a book if they so desired. Thus the farmer with $150 to spend distanced himself from those who were simply eking out an existence on the soil or from those who had just arrived in the area and had no means to pay for space in such a book and had little stake yet, in the community. The businessman, too, was able to show his worth, display his lineage, and purchase a form of everlasting advertising.

The history offered in these publishers' ventures was standardized fare, as the tables of contents testify. They were virtually interchangeable, and the biographical inclusions, whether the subject lived in Suffolk, St. Louis, or San Francisco, were much the same. Indiana folklorist Richard Dorson has pointed out that county histories from the northeast

> told one rigid, undeviating story. They began with a reference to Indians and the wilderness topography; hailed the first settlers; noted the first churches, the first schools, the first stores; devoted a chapter to the Revolution and the local "patriots"; swung into full stride with the establishment of the newspaper, the militia, the fire department, and the waterworks; rhapsodized about the fraternal lodges and civic organizations; recounted the prominent citizens of the community, and enumerated famous personages (chiefly Washington and Lafayette) who had passed through; listed a roster of the Civil War dead; and rounded off the saga with descriptions of the newest edifices on Main Street.[30]

The title of Washington Frothingham's history says it all. His book was called *History of Montgomery County [New York] Embracing Early Discoveries; The Advance of Civilization; The Labors and Triumphs of Sir William Johnson; The Inception of Development of Manufacturers; With Town and Local Records; Also Military Achievements of Montgomery Patriots*. This, historian Frothingham promised, was a history "of which all citizens could be proud."[31]

Women were the second group of people who moved into the world of the patrician historian. In 1883, the Association of Collegiate Alumnae suggested avenues of activity other than teaching that were appropriate for women, and local history was included among them. Prior to the 1880s, there were few local histories written by women. In New York State, of all the nineteenth-century histories I have surveyed, I could find only two women authors; in Iowa, there was one. The *Vermont Gazetteer*, created over the last half of the nineteenth century and edited by a woman, had but one woman author among all those who wrote town histories. David Russo, in his sweeping review of local history, found but two women in New England writing prior to the Civil War and few after that.[32] From the 1880s onward, although slowly at first, women could be found involving themselves with local history until eventually they became its primary keepers—if not authors. It has been estimated that of the 1,300 local historians who today are listed by New York's State Department of Education, 80 percent are women, and most of them over the age of fifty-five.[33]

In the past it was true that when women entered a field, such as teaching or typewriting, a devaluation of prestige and monetary return often followed. There was never much—if any—money to be made by local historians; local history would not derive esteem from the money it generated. Its regard came because of the connection local history made with place, with "old times and values," and because of the local status of its early practitioners. As most editors, publishers, and lawyers eased out of the field, the rising prestige of their own professions left with them—leaving commercial publishers, with their compilers, printers, and pressmen, and women. Thus in the early years of the twentieth century, local history underwent something of a decline in prestige: it was feminized and commercialized. In addition, the errors of its past caused the public to regard local history with less favor. Russell Headley, whose own work promised to "hue [sic] straight to the line," wrote in 1908: "It is a well-known fact that considerable prejudice exists among a great body of the people toward county histories in general, for the reason that some such compilations in the past, have been composed of fact and fiction so intermingled, as to render it a difficult matter to know what was true and what was false."[34]

Other significant factors were also at work to accelerate the decline of interest in local history during the century's early years, for the United States was undergoing rapid change. The automobile altered transportation patterns and much, much more. World War I opened to Americans a vision of a life beyond the ocean; the 1920s roared for change and mocked the tyranny and mustiness of the past. Nothing could have been more old-fashioned, more passé, more out of date than local history. Malcolm Cowley complained in his memoir that education in his youth (circa 1916) was aimed at "destroying whatever roots we had in the soil, toward eradicating our local and regional peculiarities, toward making us homeless citizens."[35] Cowley believed that only southerners retained any sense of place. "We were divested of our pride," for students, he observed, studied every history but that of where they were—a prejudice, he insisted, that existed in public schools and in universities alike.[36] George Callcott noted, on the question of teaching local history that "the subject of local history was never really popular in the schools despite state loyalty and even state laws." While a few states recommended local history in the public schools, it was not until a few decades later that it became a requirement, in many states, put in place to teach citizenship.[37]

As widespread popular interest in local history dwindled, most of those nineteenth-century commercial publishers withdrew from the field. Getting local history published became a more difficult task. Historical societies sometimes picked up the cost, but more often an author paid for the publication of his or her own book or a local printer offered copies in the hope of recovering his investment. These were expedients, however; the former perhaps more acceptable than the latter. As one indication of this trend, J. Franklin Jameson wrote James Truslow Adams about a woman from central New York who had asked how to go about having a book of local history published. Adams was at a loss for an answer: his own first book had been privately printed, and his second, a history of Southampton, New York, was "brought out for his own profit by the local printer who had printed the first one." Adams cautioned that the locale of the history might make a book more commercially acceptable. If, he suggested, the community is like Concord, Massachusetts, with an interest in history and a built-in tourist trade, the book might do well, and a publisher might be found. For a less notable place, he had slim hopes.[38]

At this point we find yet another type of individual interested in local history. Printers, pressmen, town clerks, and postal carriers, during the 1920s and 1930s, began to put their names on books and pamphlets of local history. I cannot document this trend with absolute numbers, but I have collected the names and biographies of several of these individuals and have indications of others. One was Uri Mulford, who in 1920 published lists of marriages, births, deaths, and past events as a history of Corning, New York. In the introduction to this book, Mulford, whose education and position in society were far from those held by our patrician historians of the previous century, stated boldly:

> This book was written, the type set, the pages made ready for the press, and the printing done on his own press, by Uri Mulford. If I had not devoted a great deal of time during nearly a score of years, to research work, and had not purchased the printing equipment necessary to produce these pages, this unique, authentic and comprehensive history, *Pioneer Days and Later Times in Corning and Vicinity* could not by any possibility have been produced. The cost of production would have been prohibitive. The major factor in the success of the project, however, was my skill as a master printer—a craft that I have followed with minor periods of interruption for a full half-century.[39]

Another among this group of pressmen believed that footnotes impeded or intimidated the ordinary reader and refused to allow them in the pamphlets he produced. He wanted to entertain the public by using the materials of local history. He cared very much that people know about the history of the place where they lived, and he believed that it mattered not a whit if the stories were historically accurate or could be traced through scholarly apparatus. Another member of this group, when asked why he chased down bits of the past, replied that he was interested in preserving little items about common people "for Posterity."

"Does it really matter?" asked the reporter interviewing him. He "looked genuinely surprised. He was silent for a moment, peering over his gold-rim glasses. 'Don't you think other people will enjoy it?'"[40]

Much of this discussion has been based on materials and incidents from the eastern portion of the United States, which is not to imply that local history was not written or sought in other places. In New Mexico, Pérez de Villagra published his verse epic *Historia de la Nueva México* about the exploits of Juan de Oñate in 1610. That was followed by several other Spanish-language histories over the next century. There were histories of Canadian provinces prior to confederation in 1867. In California, Hubert Howe Bancroft left his business interests in 1868, devoting himself to amassing a historical library and publishing venture. He commissioned thirty-nine histories about counties and states from Central America to Alaska by using historians and compiling histories of the development of the west and a significant collection that became the basis for the H. H. Bancroft Library at the University of California. Professional historians, of course, did not completely ignore local history. From time to time, the American Historical Association studied the issue of local history and debated the association's responsibility for and relationship to it. At its 1914 meeting, a committee of the Mississippi Valley Historical Association offered seven reasons why state universities should offer courses in state or local history. It was, according to the report, a state university's obligation to advance learning and promote culture; states owed something to history and were under an obligation to preserve their own; courses in state and local history were considered more appropriate for graduate than for undergraduate students because "other things than state and local history are more likely to be conducive to a student's culture, to his training, to his higher education." In addition, a state university should be ready and willing to lend aid and cooperation to the agencies within the state for promotion of public interest and knowledge concerning state history; the university should collect and publish materials pertaining to state history, and these activities should be under the auspices of departments of history; and—last—research in state and local history was a rich field for graduate students as an exercise in how to do history, especially because local studies could be viewed as useful to national historians.[41]

A representative to the first International Local History conference at the Institute for Historical Study at London University in 2009, from the University of North Dakota, complained about local and academic historians' lack of interaction. He noted that in many states, university people and historical society folks rarely came in contact, nor was local history much valued in the academy: "In outer darkness are the people interested in state history." He also noted that professors of history would have to learn how to deal with people who carry history around in their heads, either as participants or as descendants. In addition, a professor would have to learn how to interview "to obtain valuable historical information" and professors would need to understand that "the folks will haze him if possible as being an easy mark." He did note that state history would guarantee a writer a large audience, although those most interested would be "the pioneers of the state" and probably not any others. The role of graduate students would be to gain access for the professor "to the people."[42]

It was in the public schools where local history was to be located. Beginning in the 1930s, and after the end of World War II, local history was often an option in senior high for students who needed extra credits or a local history project was sometimes proffered for students interested in history. As the years passed, however, local history descended into the grade schools, and for the most part, in the recent past, local history—if it has been in the schools at all—has been offered to fourth graders. The trend now, in the twenty-first century, however, seems to be to abandon local history, sometimes in favor of state history. The reason for this is not that state history is more important or easier or even more appropriate for fourth-grade students but, rather, that state history, it is believed, can be tested by means of an exam, whereas local history cannot.

During the twentieth century, local history began to appear in one of its most popular and effective forms. Newspaper writers of the 1930s—and continuing to this day—seized on local events as interesting material for feature articles and weekly columns. Local history had appeared in newspapers before, of course, but mostly in the form of reminiscences, letters, and sometimes as the result of interviews with aged or notable people—or survivors of earlier times or startling events. On occasion, a newspaper would publish a document that surfaced, and, of course, newspapers noted the anniversaries of community institutions; of the founding, of business, church, school, or store beginnings and grown, and sometimes of their decline. Newspapers, of course, charted disasters.

The appearance of local history in 1930s newspapers took a slightly new form, however. Journalists who reveled in an anecdote, a joke, or a regional dialect would take a story, polish it, and present it to the paper's readers. Their interest was in the telling of highly specific tales, developing a form of local-color writing, which they did with verve. The demands that these journalists faced included the needs of editors to fill space with local, particular, "upbeat," hometown material; the pressures of a deadline; and the desire to amuse or entertain and engage readers. Ultimately, these writers were trying to sell newspapers and maintain reader loyalty. Such newspaper writers were, and continue to be, very influential. They told pieces of a community's past in its most readily available form and in an entertaining fashion. Some of their stories are insightful—important additions to an area's knowledge of its own past—some are less so. The writers' purpose was to take local history out of the hands of those who had made it dull and wearisome, to democratize it, and eventually to commercialize it. As one of them wrote: "But what about the self-trumpeted historians who are determined to keep history for the few by locking it up except on appointed occasions or deliberately making it dull?" He stormed on: "A few of us are trying to make . . . history more alive than it was made for us." When asked whether his work was fact or fiction, he said he didn't care a whit as long as it was read. That, of course, is an entirely different object than the goal of most local historians.[43]

These journalist/writers were determined to inject some vitality into history, and they did. Their newspaper columns were popular then, and similar ones continue to be today. Not only did the public get a snappy story to accompany the news and sports, readers also acquired a notion of what local history could and should be. Local history was considered a source of local entertainment, as well as a source of local pride. Readers also came to expect that local tales had a shape, a beginning, middle and end, and that they all hooked seamlessly together: history, of course, is not always like that, for it requires explanations and encounters blank places where documents do not exist, and historians cannot dance nimbly past the parts that don't fit or might not please the public.

The ways of doing local history in the past have been as varied as the reasons for writing local history. Older histories established patterns that amateur historians and the public have accepted as suitable for the genre. W. G. Hoskins, an influential English historian, noted in 1967 that, "in trying to guide local historians into the paths of righteousness and away from the amateurish imbecilities that often marked much of their work in the past, I am in danger of taking all the pleasure out of local history."[44] To change the format is often to lose the very people for whom one is writing; today newspaper writers presenting history in the popular press are among the few writing history likely to attract a broad array of local readers.

While the topics deemed suitable for history have expanded over the years, the topics ignored by local historians have remained fairly constant. Local historians have been, on the whole, antimodern; they have been overly concerned with beginnings and with the distribution of land, without looking carefully at the recent past or their own times. Local historians have rarely touched on topics that concern change, especially alterations brought about by technology, or ecological change, or the diversification of the population. As time has gone by, our local histories have repeated themselves—often to the point of reprinting earlier versions outright, without correction or addition. The table of contents of a book of local history published in 1950 is similar to one from the 1850s, with only a few new chapters added to account for the additional years. The outlook is similar from one century to the next, and the historical method used in 1950 was much the same as that used a century earlier. The motives of authors of local histories remained constant, too, and local histories at mid-twentieth century reflected historical patterns of the previous century, with little regard to advances or changes in historical linking and methodology.[45]

There were, however, during this time significant developments in the historical profession, some of which began to make an impression on local historians. An early inroad into local history by academic historians began in the 1930s with the development of a subdiscipline called "urban history." Moving away from political and economic history on a national scale, some academic historians embarked on studies of America's urban centers. They looked at sources local historians had long used and others that local historians had neglected; and they produced studies that asked about change over time, that sought to identify the continuities that persisted despite a community's growth. Urban studies looked in particular at how our idea of community has grown, how institutions have expanded and public services, such as police, water and electricity, have created the world we have inherited. Blake McKelvey's studies of Rochester, New York, are models of this genre. Constance McLaughlin Green, another urban historian, wrote as early as 1940 that history "from the bottom up" (her phrase) needed to look at various aspects of community life, to explain what happened (and where and when) as well as why. She complained that most of the local histories she had seen were written for community self-glorification, were antiquarian, lacked perspective, and were dull. She recommended that local historians study the field methods of the sociologist and read cultural anthropology in order to gain a broader understanding of history and historical methods. In 1940, Green called for studies of nondominant groups in a community, of class antagonisms, and of the emergence of social responsibility.[46] Such studies require careful use of historical documents, of course, and a respect for what emerges from them. Merle Curti wrote that he saw the need

> for cultural histories of communities: studies that would yield information about the backgrounds and education of settlers and later citizens; cleavages in communities and their various effects upon community institutions; the roles played by church, school and press; the forces, too little studied, which differentiate one community from another; and the relations of Main Street to the world.

Curti also noted that "here the vigorous local interest that is sometimes channeled into antiquarian backwaters can join deep historical currents."[47]

The work of Green and Curti and other urban historians (whose important research continues to this day) has had relatively little impact on local historians. One academic historian told me recently that only three copies of his important study of one community, which is frequently quoted in academic literature, had been sold in that place, yet it is now considered something of a classic and is read by most graduate students in American history. Local historians tend to continue in established patterns, their history rich with detail, quaint ways, and sayings, their readers content. In 1950, Richard Shryock noted that two types of historiography had developed in the United States. "The professionals," he wrote, "were concerned with over-all developments and interpretations; the local historians with a summary of the facts." He observed that local historians tended to be interested in "everything which had happened just because it had happened." I would have to dispute this for if anything, local historians are very close to the facts available in their home place.[48]

An institutional link between local historians and the history professionals was formed with the birth, in 1940, of the American Association for State and Local History. That organization has advanced the cause of local history and its practitioners in a variety of ways, although its focus is more clearly on historical organizations and their needs than on those who research and write local history. Today, the greatest potential bonds among the various workers in Clio's field are a new wave of interest in local historical studies on the part of academic historians and a new sense of purpose among local historians. The "new" social history has spread into many areas of academic historical work and its research materials are to be found in America's localities, and it has the potential to interest both groups of historians. Its researchers turn to local archives and to questions of a demographic nature in order to know the past more fully. New studies of mobility, religion, population, race, gender, class, and family life have opened up new historical questions and exciting ways of seeking answers.[49]

This "new" social history did not spring into being without antecedents. Its origins can be found in the work of American urban historians and among historians abroad. In England, academic interest in local history in the later 1950s culminated with the establishment at the University of Leicester of a Chair of English Local History. Interested in the origin, rise, and decline of communities, the Leicester School sought to encourage careful, thoughtful work by amateurs and professionals alike. Today, British social historians have expanded on the outlook of the Leicester School and embarked on broader demographic studies of English life in the past. Local history has been taught in a number of colleges, and there are two local history journals that address the needs and concerns of amateur historians. But the last quarter of the twentieth century might have been an apex, for in this new century, there has been a decline in Great Britain as elsewhere in the teaching and support for local history.[50]

In France, the route to local history came in the form of demographic studies rooted in department, provincial, and church records. Researchers sought the answers to questions of national importance in local archives. Local history alone, the great French historian Marc Bloch said, "makes the study of more general problems possible."[51] Wedded to this use of sources in villages and in departmental archives was the quest for knowledge about all of society, not merely information about those people who traditionally had power and whose history has generally been written. This was history that built carefully from an economic understanding of village life by looking at all the people in the area, their system of work, and ultimately their culture. In addition, French historians attempted to understand long-range trends in population change—trends that were probably unperceived even by the participants themselves. These gigantic studies were ultimately made possible by limiting the area in which the researcher worked: that is, the geographic area of the study put reasonable limits on questions about the nature of life in the past. The computer became the technological assistant that made it possible to deal with such vast quantities of material in new and sophisticated ways. For example, *Enduring Memory: Time and History in a French Village* by Françoise Zonabend focuses on the rituals and patterns of daily life and has a great deal to teach American local historians by suggesting topics and methods of doing local history.[52]

In the United States, the "new" social history borrowed from these foreign trends and adapted them to the types of information and questions important in this country. During the 1970s and 1980s, there was some academic interest in local history, but that does not in any way account for local history's new popularity with the general public. In the 1970s, the country experienced *Roots*, the Foxfire series of books that focused on traditional life and folkways, and the architectural preservation movement that touched so many of our cities and towns. In addition, the national celebration of the Bicentennial of the American Revolution took place, in its most meaningful form, in America's hometowns. Just as during the period of the centennial celebration in 1876, the bicentennial stressed our hometown heritage, and with it came an outpouring of interest in local history. A new crop of books of local history emerged. Many were simply reprints of older, nineteenth-century histories, but some were new works of history written by local authors.

Commercial publishers once again appeared. The most prominent is Arcadia Press, interested in publishing short, well-illustrated, and chronologically balanced town and city and village histories in their "Cities of America" series. The press expanded to African American history, sports, and organizational history. After identifying an author, Arcadia editors provided guidelines, page limits, standards for picture quality, a rather tight but realistic timeline from the date a contract was signed to publication, and even royalties to the author or supporting institution. These books, all in a familiar brown cover, proved to be immediately identifiable, and very popular with the public. Uneven in quality, as any large series of books might be, Arcadia tapped into an interest in knowing about one's hometown or places one visited. This format can also be seen in several other presses, including The History Press (with which I have published).

Over time, local history has formed, developed, re-formed, expanded in outlook, and come of age. Its past bequeathed certain patterns, and it took from each era characteristics that have marked it well. Over time, for many reasons, it moved from the shadows into a commanding position in many of our states and cities, counties and towns.

NOTES

1. H. P. R. Finberg, "Local History," in *Approaches to History* (London: Routledge and Kegan Paul, 1962), 125.

2. Anthony Richard Wagner, *English Genealogy* (Oxford: Clarendon Press, 1972), 367; H. P. R. Finberg, "Local History," in Approaches to History, ed. H. P. R. Finberg (London: Routledge and Kegan Paul, 1962), 111–25; W. G. Hoskins, *Local History in England* (London: Longmans, 1959), especially chap. 2; W. R. Powell, "Local History in Theory and Practice," *Bulletin of the Institute of Historical Research* 31 (1958): 41–48; Pierre Goubert, "Local History," *Daedalus* 100 (Winter 1971): 113–27. See also the Rev. Thomas Dunham Whitaker, *History and Antiquities of Craven*, 2nd ed. (London: J. Nichols and Son, 1812), v, quoted in Wagner, *English Genealogy*, 381.

3. Hermann E. Ludewig, *The Literature of American Local History* (New York: privately printed, 1846), vii. David J. Russo has written an important account of the amateur writers of our country's history; see *Keepers of Our Past: Local Historical Writing in the United States, 1820s–1930s* (New York: Greenwood Press, 1988). Russo deals with the early antiquarians, the emergence of town and city historians, the formulas used by local historians, and the problem of local historians and academic practitioners of history.

4. John Higham, *The Reconstruction of American History* (New York: Harper and Brothers, 1962), 10–11. Not all these patrician historians were men. See Deborah Pitman Clifford, *The Passion of Abby Hemenway: Memory, Spirit, and the Making of History* (Montpelier: Vermont Historical Society, 2001).

5. H. C. Goodwin, *Pioneer History of Courtland County and the Border Wars of New York* (New York: A. B. Burdick Publisher, 1859), 94. See, especially, Russo, *Keepers of Our Past*. Russo worked from the Library of Congress local history collection to study the phasing of local history in the United States.

6. Franklin B. Hough, *History of Lewis County in the State of New York from the Beginning of Its Settlement to the Present Time* (Albany: Munsell and Rowland, 1860), 1.

7. Horace King, *Early History of Ithaca: A Lecture* (Ithaca: Mack Andrus and Co. Printers, 1847), 18.

8. Appleton Prentiss Clark Griffin, *Index of American Local History in Collections Published in 1890–95* (Boston: Carl H. Heintzemann, 1896), throughout; for almanacs and anniversary speeches, see Ludewig, *The Literature of American Local History,* especially 111–17. The term "oral history" was first used in Vermont in 1863 when Winslow Watson, speaking before Historical Society, complained that much of the local history of the state was older residents who remembered it died. "I have been amazed," Watson declared,

"by observing in my own local researches, the ravages made by a single decade among the fountains of oral history in a community" (in Clifford, *The Passion of Abby Hemenway*, 224).

9. J. Cooper, *The Chronicles of Cooperstown* (Cooperstown, NY: H. E. Phinney, 1838); J. B. Wilkerson, *Annals of Binghamton* (Binghamton, NY: Times Association, [1840] 1872), iii–iv.

10. Louis Bisceglia, "Writers of Small Histories: Local Historians in the United States and Britain," *The Local Historian* 14 (February 1980): 4–10. The term "small histories" originated with Dr. Samuel Johnson. See, too, John Delafield, "A General View and Agricultural Survey of the County of Seneca," *Transactions of the New York State Agricultural Society 1850* X (1851): 397; and Nathaniel S. Prime, *History of Long Island from Its First Settlement to the Year 1845 with Special Reference to Its Ecclesiastical Concerns* (New York: R. Carter, 1845), 111.

11. Wilkerson, *Annals of Binghamton*, v.

12. George H. Callcott, *History in the United States 1800–1860: Its Practice and Purpose* (Baltimore: Johns Hopkins University Press, 1970), 87–88.

13. David D. Van Tassel, "Biography: The Creation of National Heroes, 1776–1849," in *Recording America's Past: An Interpretation of the Development of Historical Studies in America 1607–1884* (Chicago: University of Chicago Press, 1960), 66–67.

14. Washington Irving, *Knickerbocker's History of New York* (New York: G. P. Putnam's Sons, [1894] 1908), 1:23–25.

15. John Higham, *Writing American History* (Bloomington: Indiana University Press, 1970), 5.

16. Wilkerson, *Annals of Binghamton*, iv.

17. Walter Muir Whitehill, *Independent Historical Societies* (Lunenburg, VT: Boston Athenaeum, 1962), 350; and Van Tassel, *Recording America's Past*, appendix, 181–90, in which there is a list of historical societies and the dates of their creation.

18. D. H. H., *History of Clinton and Franklin Counties* (Philadelphia: J. W. Lewis Co., 1880), preface; Nathan Bouton, *Festal Gatherings of the Early Settlers and Present Inhabitants of Virgil* (Dryden, NY: A. M. Ford, 1878), 2:1.

19. Gilbert W. Hazeltine, *The Early History of the Town of Ellicott, Chautauqua County, N.Y., Compiled Largely from the Personal Recollections of the Author* (Jamestown, NY: Lewis Historical Publishing Co., 1887), v–vi. H. J. Swinney brought this particular history to my attention.

20. Higham, *The Reconstruction of American History*, 10–11; Van Tassel, "Denouement: The Triumph of National History, 1876–84," in *Recording America's Past*, 179.

21. John Higham, "Herbert Baxter Adams and the Study of Local History," *American Historical Review* 89 (December 1984): 1225–39.

22. Higham, "Herbert Baxter Adams and the Study of Local History," 1232.

23. J. Franklin Jameson to John Jameson, January 5, 1889, quoted in Higham, "Herbert Baxter Adams and the Study of Local History," 1232. And see Russo, *Keepers of Our Past*, chap. 12, "Amateurs and Academics," 191–204.

24. Edward Eggleston, quoted in Higham, "Herbert Baxter Adams and the Study of History," 1232; and Larry E. Tise, "State and Local History: A Future from the Past," *The Public Historian* 1 (Summer 1979): 15.

25. George W. Cowles, *Landmarks of Wayne County, New York* (Syracuse: D. Mason and Co., 1895); Edgar C. Emerson, ed., *Our County and Its People: A Descriptive Work on Jefferson County, New York* (Boston: Boston History Co. Publishers, 1898), iii–v; Washington Frothingham, *History of Montgomery County, Embracing Early Discoveries . . .* (Syracuse: D. Mason and Co., 1892), 7.

26. Christfield Johnson, *Centennial History of Erie County, New York* (Buffalo: Mathews and Warren, 1876), 7.

27. Franklin B. Hough, *History of Lewis County, New York* (Syracuse: Mason and Co., 1883); John A. Haddock, *The Growth of a Century as Illustrated in the History of Jefferson County, New York, from 1793 to 1894* (Philadelphia: Sherman and Co., 1894); Arad Thomas, *Pioneer History of Orleans County, New York* (Albion, NY: H. A. Bruner, Orleans Steam Press, 1871), iv–v.

28. H. P. Smith, *History of Cortland County, New York* (Syracuse: D. Mason and Co., 1885), 3. See Russo, *Keepers of Our Past*, chap. 9, "Local History as a Publishing Venture," 149–64.

29. Harold Nestler, *Bibliography of New York State Communities, Counties, Towns, Villages* (Port Washington, NY: Ira J. Friedman, 1968), foreword.

30. Richard M. Dorson, *American Folklore and the Historian* (Chicago: University of Chicago Press, 1971), 149.

31. Washington Frothingham, *History of Montgomery County [New York] Embracing Early Discoveries; The Advance of Civilization; The Labors and Triumphs of Sir William Johnson; The Inception of Development of Manufacturers; With Town and Local Records; Also Military Achievements of Montgomery Patriots* (Syracuse, 1892), 7.

32. See Clifford, *The Passion of Abby Hemenway*, 95–96; and Russo, *Keepers of Our Past*, 27–28. For a history of British women writers of local history, see, too, Joan Thirsk, "Women Local and Family Historians," in *Oxford Companion to Local and Family History*, ed. David Hey (Oxford: Oxford University Press, 1996), 498–504.

33. Marion Talbot, "Report of the Association of Collegiate Alumnae," in *Worlds Congress of Representative Women*, ed. May Wright Sewall (Chicago: Rand, McNally and Co., 1894), 793. See also Joan J. Brumberg and Nancy Tomes, "Women in the Professions: A Research Agenda for American Historian," *Reviews in American History* 10 (June 1982): 285–86. In 1999 the acting New York State historian compiled a report entitled "Statistics from the 1998 Annual Report of the Local Government Historians of New York State," in which he found that of the historians who responded to the questionnaire, over 60 percent were women. It is unlikely that this figure has changed significantly.

34. Russel Headley, *History of Orange County, New York* (Middletown, NY: Van Deusen and Elms, 1908), 5.

35. Malcolm Cowley, *Exile's Return: A Narrative of Ideas* (New York: Norton, 1934), 3.

36. Cowley, *Exile's Return*, 31.

37. Callcott, *History in the United States 1800–1860*, 90.

38. J. Franklin Jameson to James Truslow Adams, March 1, 1918, J. Franklin Jameson Papers, Box 46, Library of Congress; James Truslow Adams, letter to J. Franklin Jameson, March 5, 1918, J. Franklin Jameson Papers, Box 46, Library of Congress.

39. Uri Mulford, *Pioneer Days and Later Times in Corning and Vicinity, 1789–1920* (Corning, NY: U. Mulford Publisher, 1920), preface.

40. See "Historian Man of Year," *The Ithaca Journal*, January 2, 1980. See also Helen Hooven Santmyer, *Ohio Town: A Portrait of Xenia* (New York: Harper and Row, 1984), 255–56.

41. "Meeting of the American Historical Association in Chicago," *American Historical Review* 20 (1915): 518–19.

42. "Meeting of the American Historical Association in Chicago," 518.

43. Henry Charlton Beck, *More Forgotten Towns of Southern New Jersey* (Rahway, NJ: Quinn and Boden Co., 1936), 6.

44. W. G. Hoskins, *Fieldwork in Local History* (London: Faber and Faber, 1967).

45. John D. Haskell Jr., "Writings on Maine History: The Story up to Now," paper presented at a symposium on Maine history, Orono, Maine, May 5, 1978; R. Richard Wohl and A. Theodore Brown, "The Usable Past: A Study of Historical Traditions in Kansas City," *Huntington Library Quarterly* 23 (May 1960): 237–59, reprinted in *The Pursuit of Local History: Readings on Theory and Practice*, ed. Carol Kammen (Walnut Creek, CA: AltaMira Press, 1996), 145–63.

46. See Bruce M. Stave, *The Making of Urban History: Historiography through Oral History* (Beverly Hills: Sage Publications, 1977), especially interviews with Blake McKelsey and Constance McLaughlin Green, 33–62, 203–344. See also Constance McLaughlin Green, "The Value of Local History," in *The Cultural Approach to History*, ed. Caroline F. Ware (New York: Columbia University Press, 1940), 275–90.

47. Merle Curti, in Theodore C. Blegan, *Grass Roots History* (Minneapolis: University of Minnesota Press, 1947), 247.

48. Whitfield J. Bell Jr., "The Amateur Historian," *New York History* 8 (July 1972): 265–82, reprinted in *The Pursuit of Local History*, 21–32; Richard Shryock, "Changing Perspectives in Local History," *New York History* 31 (July 1950): 243–60.

49. Lawrence Stone, "English and United States Local History," *Daedalus* 100 (Winter 1971): 128–32.

50. Finberg, "Local History"; Powell, "Local History in Theory and Practice"; Alan Rogers, "The Study of Local History—Opinion and Practice 3. New Horizons in Local History," *The Local Historian* 12 (June 1976): 67–73; Hoskins, *Local History in England*; David Iredale, *Local History Research and Writing: A Manual for Local History Writers* (Leeds: Elmfield Press, 1974).

51. Marc Bloch, *The Ile-de-France: The Country around Paris* (Ithaca: Cornell University Press, 1971), 120.

52. Goubert, "Local History," 113–27; Françoise Zonabend, *Enduring Memory: Time and History in a French Village*, trans. Anthony Forster (Manchester: Manchester University Press, 1984).

Coda to Chapter 1

Revising What Is Held as True

The artifacts of the past can have a way of making us uncomfortable. We encounter in the local historical past evidence of other ways of thinking that are quite out of step with our own. In our concern for fairness and inclusion—some will call this political correctness—these encounters may become problematic. We discover when we stop to read them that some of our historical markers are wrong, others skewed; that some place-names reflect the past as it used to be discussed, not as we today would prefer to discuss or think about it; and that public monuments reflect a particular, exclusive past without consideration of how others might view them. Sanford Levinson, in his book *Written in Stone: Public Monuments in Changing Societies*,[1] discusses a number of interesting topics such as the Confederate generals who stride on horseback down Monument Avenue in Richmond, Virginia, a city with a large African American population; the Memorial to the Confederate Dead located on the statehouse grounds in Austin, Texas; and the Liberty Monument in New Orleans that recalls the 1874 takeover of the Louisiana government by members of the White League. These are but a few of the pieces of public statuary erected in one era that make us wince. Levinson quotes Kirk Savage: "A public monument represents a kind of collective recognition—in short, legitimacy—for the memory deposited there." Statues do not, he insists, "arise as if by natural law."[2] What they do, however, is confront us with an uncomfortable past. We know how we react when politicians continue to use racial epithets or to avow unscientific ideas that collide with what is known and generally believed. Levinson discusses the present-day display of the Confederate flag, flying over three statehouses.

Levinson's examples range from Eastern Europe, where regimes have changed public statues to suit the current climate, to the Shaw Memorial on Boston Common and the Suffrage Statue recently brought up from the basement to the Rotunda of the Capitol. His concern, however, is primarily with the American South.

His book reminds me that those of us involved in local or regional history have relics from the past that also cause us difficulty. For example, we all recognize that there is bias in our archival holdings. Most of the records that were sought and collected, those that form the basis of local or regional collections and, indeed, most of what local history once was, stem from and document a community's elite—or its emerging elite: or at least the literate whose families preserved documents. These were the commercially successful, the socially prominent, the upwardly mobile, and those participating in community institutions. Most of the story we have to tell from our collected treasures is about the white upper classes, and most generally males.

We have responded and consciously expanded beyond this base, finding new ways to use the materials that are already in our collections, seeing some old materials in new ways, and seeking additions to the archive of documents more representative of all the people of the past. Even old curmudgeons have changed their tune and cease to call that box of women's diaries "dull stuff." They have begun to regard a variety of source material with something akin to appreciation, if not fondness. We have found ways to overcome the problem of what an archive holds.

But still, local history, now and again, is apt to reach out and tweak us. Driving along a highway, we pass historical markers replete with messages that reflect a particular view of the past. Those markers were erected, for the most part, for centennial observations during the latter part of the nineteenth century or at the dawn of the age of automobile travel and the development of tourism during the first three decades of the twentieth. They reflect the historical concerns of those who had the interest and were in the best position to see that the markers were put in place. Thus, there is a bias toward old families or, in my part of the country, to families connected one way or another to the Daughters of the American Revolution who wrote the marker text and paid for the installations.

Newer highway markers reflect the historical fashions of our own time, so that, all over the country, we encounter monuments that reflect history's latest concerns, such as African American or women's history, and we have in many instances corrected the side-of-the-road history of Native Americans. This righting of the record reflects our need to be inclusive of aspects and people of the past who were once ignored. We all owe James W. Loewen a debt of gratitude for his book *Lies Across America: What our Historic Sites Get Wrong*, first published in 1999 by the New Press in New York. Loewen takes on the myths we perpetuate and urges us to get them right, to explain those that remain, and to think about what our roadside signs commemorate today. This is a book that everyone should read.

Place-names, especially those of geographic features, can also bring us up short. This is true of Massacre Lake in Nevada and Massacre Rock in Idaho—or even "Niggerhead," mentioned by the Governor of Texas. Located along Interstate 15, Massacre Rock in Idaho commemorates an Indian raid made on passing emigrants in 1862. Well, we know now, from the work of a number of historians, that this might or might not have been what happened and that most "massacres" were hardly that. "Massacre," of course, worries us because of how the word has been used to place blame on Native Americans for events that were usually pitched battles between adversaries. We recognize today that there is more than one way to look at a historical event.

Reversing how we think about an event or person of the past has always happened. Take the case of Dr. Mary Walker. Born in 1832 in Oswego County, New York, she attended local schools and then the Syracuse Medical College, graduating in 1855. She married, though she did not adopt her husband's name, and the couple practiced medicine together for several years until they separated. Dr. Walker had always been interested in dress reform; she wore the Bloomer outfit for a time and then settled into the habit of wearing men's clothing.

At the outbreak of the Civil War, Dr. Mary Walker appeared at a field hospital in Virginia and began to work. The Confederacy accused her of acting as a Union spy because of her many trips through the lines, and when captured she was sentenced to a term in the Richmond Prison. Upon her release, Dr. Walker continued to serve as a medical officer, even in the face of complaints by Union doctors who did not want to work alongside a woman. In 1865 she was awarded the Congressional Medal of Honor for Meritorious Service.

Yet in 1917 a federal board of review decided that the citation had been unwarranted and that claims of her heroism were untrue. Her medal was officially withdrawn and she died two years later. By 1982, however, the historical tide had changed again, and the US Post Office issued a commemorative stamp honoring Dr. Mary Walker of Oswego. Her biography appears in *Notable American Women*. This is a woman about whom controversy swirled and whose reputation, both nationally and locally, shifted with the fashion of the times.

What do we do about parts of the past that make us uncomfortable? We cannot always remove an offending historic marker from along a roadside—nor should we in many cases—but we can erect other markers to tell more of the story than the original offers. Or, we can move an offending marker or monument to a historical society where it can be interpreted in terms of its times and how those ideas have become outmoded—and why. We can be sure to explain to the public about the changing nature of historical interpretation, about the ideas that inform the history we present, and to stress, as Carl Becker did, that history is two things: it is the past, and it is what happens in the minds of historians who bring to the documents their own interests and concerns, as well as the interests, concerns, and historical understandings of their own eras. Thus, the history that has excited me has been about gender and democratization of opportunity, just as historians younger than I see local history as the place to explore environmentalism or other topics as they become the social questions of their own day.

It seems to me that these debates about the past are one way of teaching a public used to thinking of history as static—having learned in school that history consists of right and wrong answers—that, in fact, what we know and how we understand just about anything depends very much upon who we are and on the times in which we live. As ideas change, so too do historical fashions—not in order to dress up the truth but to better understand it.

NOTES

1. Sanford Levinson, *Written in Stone: Public Monuments in Changing Societies* (Durham, NC: Duke University Press, 1998).
2. Levinson, *Written in Stone*, 63.

Chapter Two

Thinking about History

I'm beginning to wonder should we trust historians at all!
—Hugh O'Neil, in Brian Friel's *Making History*[1]

Over the years, I have been very much influenced by three historians in particular. What each has said about history has alerted me to problems, to situations that I have eventually encountered, and they have made me aware of the consequences of what I am doing, of what I might not have seen or understood left to my own resources. Each has aided me, though none of them is responsible for my failure to adhere to their high standards. Each has caused me to think more deeply about the consequences of a historian's actions. Two of these historians are long dead; my husband more recently and I hope you will encounter his many books on your own. His interests were broad; overall, he is remembered for his wit, his concern with how Americans have faced who they were, and how they have remembered who we once were. He dealt with memory, most especially: how we talk about the past, what we say, and why. The other two historians I revere are Carl Becker and Marc Bloch.

I could not have had better companions for the doing of history, and I would like to send you to their works: "Everyman His Own Historian," in Carl Becker's book of essays by the same name, and *The Historian's Craft* by Marc Bloch. Their messages stand up well over time.[2] Becker is well known to every American historian though possibly less well today as historical fashions change and other historical gurus come along, as many have. Becker also wrote notable local history. Especially important is his essay entitled "Kansas" in *Everyman His Own Historian*, and there is also his book about New York politics in the period just prior to the revolutionary war. Marc Bloch, one of the founders of the French Annales School, was killed by the German SS in 1944. He wrote a book of local history called *Ile-de-France: The Country around Paris*.[3] Both of these men wrote with startling clarity about the craft of history; each knew what local history is all about, and each thought that local history could adhere to and represent the highest of historical standards. There are other historians I also admire, but I carry with me the words of these three. Each has written with a beauty that illuminates what he has to say. If you have read Becker and Bloch, then you can skip this chapter. If you have read them, and continue reading here, you will understand my debt to them and to others.

Carl Becker commented wisely that history is two things. History is the past itself—that is, the events that happened some time ago. But it is something else, he observed, for history is also what happens in the mind of the historian. Historians look for two things when contemplating the past: we look for that which has changed and that which has remained constant. A flood changes things; the river with its possibilities for good and harm remains constant. Town government is a constant; misuse of the town road fund is a point of change, as is the decision to open agricultural land to development for housing. When we identify change we ask a batch of questions: Why did this happen, how did the change come about, who or what triggered an event, what were the consequences of that change—on the subject itself or on parts of it, on those involved, on those watching from the sidelines? How did people react; what did they do differently because of it; what did they miss?

If it is an institution under investigation, we must wonder why it has remained, what temptations or forces altered it or failed to do so, what sorts of things happened because of its constancy. A town board might be considered an example of an ongoing entity important for the governance it provides through the actions of those five or seven people who run the community and gain their position by election or appointment. The town board, however, also changes its functions as dictated by popular demand, by the availability of funds and their source, by state and federal mandate, and by the times in which it functions or that which the public needs or demands. So something continuous can also change over time.

If we look at something that changed—a local boundary relocated, the switch of a church from one denomination to another, the failure of a company, or someone who acted and made a difference—in each case, the change occurred from within and from without, and the causes need to be explored. Yet we also remember that, even with change, there are things that remain constant: the church continues to serve a congregation (although it might be a different group of people or even a different creed); the company might reorganize or be bought out by another; individuals might become wealthy and therefore do things out of the ordinary, yet they will also remain themselves. We need to explore the role of the government, or company, or church—what precipitated change, what resisted change, and what forced the issue. Then we need to consider what the process of change was, how it was managed and who managed it, and what the costs were.

I am alert to change but wary too. I am always caught up short when someone says that the twentieth century dawned and therefore things changed. Well yes, the date changed, but if what you mean by the twentieth century is modernization, a new age, or scientific times, you will find that those things happened piecemeal, a bit here and something there, but not all at once everywhere or even anywhere. Finally, we need to wonder how that which changed was different, how it fit into the local context, and who approved, who was alienated, and who benefited. We explore everything we can about the change from one status to another, always asking the paired questions: who advocated, who didn't; who benefited, who didn't; who had influence, who didn't?

If we look for something that did not change over time, then we have to reason a bit more subtly. What does not change? Well, the land might be considered fairly constant, although over time our use of the land has changed it, the land itself can wear out, the ore underground can run out, or something can be found that no one previously knew was there. The weather, too, is always there, but we all know that there are weather patterns over a number of years, and so the weather changes. What else might not change? Well, for me the one thing that is constant is human nature. We learn more, we act differently in different times, but in so many ways human nature does not change all that much. We still have basic needs that can be identified now and in times past: we love, we create families, we are lonely, we sing and are happy, we have a need for belief in something—just what varies from person to person. We express anger, we are thoughtless, we covet, we are blind to much that is in front of us. On the other hand, we have, over time, become more tolerant of diversity, and if that is a facet of human nature, then even human nature changes. Mother love is a facet of human nature that remains constant, even while the definition of love and what it means in terms of caring for our young has changed from one period to another—just as the idea of who a mother is and what her role should or might be has changed.

What else might be constant? Well, over time we have formed local governments and we have created ways of trading goods, services, and money. We strive to be more than self-sufficient. We believe in education or improvement. So some things can be seen as the same, although they are altered by circumstances, by era, and possibly by place.

Carl Becker noted that while history is the past, it is also something else, and this is where we historians come into the picture. Becker said that history is also in the mind of the historian. What he meant is that coexisting with the past, with all its changes and constancy, there is also the history that is created in the mind. The historian, in an effort to understand the past, shapes the history of the subject in his or her mind.

It is easy to say, sure, okay, I know that. But Becker is subtle and wise. He is not only saying that we historians write the history of our communities; he is saying that we are creating what history we write in our minds. And he reminds us that the history I create in my mind is not, and can never be, quite the same as the history you create in yours. In other words, history is not a science that is replicable from one laboratory to another. History is not a formula to be tested so that each attempt will yield the same answer.

 Recorded history is, rather, what happens in the mind of the historian, and this merits our attention because each mind is different. History is an art form, and it is important to remember that if history is in the mind of the historian, then it is subject to the interests, intelligence, and even the preoccupations and era of each individual historian. And where do those interests come from? Well, obviously, some come from our own inclinations— or prejudices. I do not do railroad history, for example. I just don't much care for train lines, and locomotive types, and car numbers. So given a batch of documents about a local train line—the DL and W (the Delaware Lackawanna and Western Railroad), for example—I will look at those papers differently from someone who wants to know developments in the type of locomotives in operation, how many cars there were, and their routes. I will look at railroad documents—if you can get me to look at them at all—in terms of what impact the railroad had on a community, who used it and for what, what happened before it was there, and what happened when the railroad company abandoned the route and the community. So this other "straw" historian and I would create in our minds, and on the page, two different histories even if we used the same file of papers because we ask different questions, have different interests. And the reason is that we are two distinct individuals with our own particular interests and abilities.

So we have to ask again, where do our interests come from? Well, they come from a variety of things. My interests (and yours) come from our personalities, our background knowledge—things we have read and have been influenced by. Our interests come from our abilities: if you can read Spanish, then you can use the material written in that language that may pertain to that railroad. Because I cannot read Spanish, I will not read those documents, or I will try to find someone to read and translate them for me. So right there our abilities have created differences in how we deal with the materials in front of us. If I can make neither heads nor tails of an account book, but you can, then you will use that material differently and most likely better than I. But because I am very sympathetic to workers, when we encounter them in a strike or in a library open to workers in the evening, I might reflect their past in a more empathetic way than you.

In addition to our interests, abilities, and personalities, we are influenced by our times. When I went to college there was no women's history or black history or Indian history. Well, that is inaccurate. There has always been women's history: it is just that, until the late 1960s, no one was looking for it, looking at it, or teaching it. Just so with black history: until the civil rights movement of the 1960s, only a few people were interested in pursuing the history of African Americans. So their history was not represented in our general history courses or even in specialized courses. Today, of course, everyone is interested in class, gender, and race, so these topics are better represented. And we think about them when contemplating a topic in our local history setting for an exhibit or publication or in thinking about how to approach a history topic.

Therefore, given those railroad documents we have been talking about, one person might be interested in where the trains ran and how often, whereas another local historian today might ask questions about who the workers on the train were—if all jobs on the railroad were open to everyone who looked for work or if employment was segregated by race and gender. The times influence what we are interested in, and they influence the questions we ask about the past, just as our personalities and our interests also influence the subjects we pursue in the past.

There are problems with documents too. Events in the past were just that. They were things that happened, they were life itself as lived by others—they were not designed to be the subject of future research. All the documents we might hope to find about an event will not be there, and some of our questions about the past can never be answered. This is one way that the recorded past warps our present-day understanding. It happens in other ways too, for not all the documents created about an event may have survived, and this creates a skewed version of the past. Some of us, in addition, are better researchers than others—some are more persistent, range more widely, find ways of teasing information from sources, and so each of us gathers what there is of a past event in a different fashion. I might have a few documents; you might have many more. That difference will create different histories right there. But even if we each have identical documents in front of us, we will arrange them differently. If you and I have four documents about this awful train subject, I might ignore the account book, and you might use it; I might think the complaint by a widow whose husband was a railroad worker is important, and you might not. We will arrange the sources we find in a different order, give different emphases to one thing or another, but in general, not to the same thing. And even if we both rate one document to be of the greatest importance, because we are different individuals with different skills, interests, prejudices, and training, we will not necessarily interpret that document the same way. When we think of the questions we want to ask of the documents, you and I will ask different questions; when it comes to

writing about the episode, your ability to write well and my less able writing
will further differentiate between the histories that we two will create.

Our sources present us with problems because not every document that
might have been created was created and not every document has survived.
As researchers we find different items to use for the history we are writing.
So how we select the documents, how we arrange them, how we address
them, and how well we think and write will also cause us, or allow us, to
write different histories. "Do we need three hundred biographies of Abraham
Lincoln?" a student asked me the other day, and I responded, "Of course."
Each is different; each has a different focus; each represents a different
historian's view and ability to create a Lincoln biography.

These individual differences in who we are and the times in which we
work color the very topics we address, the sources we search for and locate,
and what we make of them. In his play *Making History*, Brian Friel has Peter
Lombard, the titular bishop of Armagh and primate of all Ireland, respond to
the question "Don't you believe in the truth, Archbishop?" by saying:

> I don't believe that a period of history—a given space of time—my life—your
> life—that it contains within it one "true" interpretation just waiting to be
> mined. But I do believe that it may contain within it several possible narra-
> tives: the life of Hugh O'Neill can be told in many different ways. And those
> ways are determined by the needs and the demands and the expectations of
> different people and different eras. What do they want to hear? How do they
> want it told? So that in a sense I am not altogether my own man, Hugh. To an
> extent I simply fulfill the needs, satisfy the expectation—don't I?[4]

Yet history does not change. That is, all the stuff of history that has survived
is always there. It is our ideas about history that change; our ideas about what
is important change, our ideas of what should be taught and known change,
as do our ideas about what to look for and even how we pose questions about
the past.

This is something that puzzles those people who went through school
taking history courses because they had to. Whether they enjoyed the subject
or not, they learned that history is full of dates that needed to be memorized
and then spouted out on standardized tests. For many of them, history is
something with prescribed answers. Those people, because they have not had
the chance to think more about history—or have not been challenged to think
about it—are uncomfortable with the idea that history is not a set piece; that
facts can be used differently, and that interpretations of history can see and
reveal things where they were not seen or understood before. When the
curators at the Smithsonian Museum on the Mall in Washington, D.C.
wanted to create an exhibit about the *Enola Gay* and the end of World War
II, controversy erupted. Many people, especially those who had fought in the
war or lived through it at home, thought of the war one way. Recent histo-

rians, on the other hand, have seen new materials from the era, and they asked new questions that caused them to regard the *Enola Gay* as a more complicated issue, not merely as an airplane that delivered the atomic bomb that brought about the end of fighting in the Pacific. In the fifty years since the bomb was used, public attitudes have changed too. But for some of the people, especially those who remembered with great relief that the war ended, or for those in harm's way, for those worried about loved ones, ending the war any way possible was what was important at the time. They are, in general, not interested in different interpretations of something they knew and suffered through. To them, to consider other viewpoints is to deny the history they hold to, the history that they lived through and consider themselves to be witnesses to and authorities on. Who are the historians who can shake that firsthand knowledge? Yet the memory they hold to is but one version of the past, incomplete then and incomplete now: skewed.

And there are still other problems when doing local history. Those documents that we rely on to tell us what happened in the past were not intended to be documents. Rather, they were letters or diaries, memoirs, or business papers or accounts. We turn them into documents when we rescue and then use them, and then we worry that they do not tell us enough. They were not, however, intended to "explain" the past to us. We have turned them from their original function to our own purposes.

There is a problem, too, when local historians look only at their own communities and see events as unique when they might not have been; they fail to see that some things are common to a region or a nation. Indeed, many local historians fail to see whether materials about a community or about an event in a community's past might not exist in a nearby archive. This causes some local historians to limit what is available to them by failing to think within a regional scope. If one researches the effects of the Great Depression in Groton, it would be smart to see what was happening in Lansing to the west and Cortland to the east. Seeing what was happening in adjacent towns gives the historian a basis for comparison. Thus it is important that a community historian read the histories of nearby communities: sometimes themes in common will appear that will enrich his or her work; sometimes it will become apparent that an event *is* unique; sometimes there will be illuminating comments to be found in neighboring places. We need to remember that though we might say we are doing the history of the Town of Caroline, people did not live their lives that way. Those in Caroline had relatives and friends elsewhere with whom they corresponded, who visited them, and who joined in their moments of celebration and sadness. The patterns of life were not lived according to geographic boundaries; neither should our histories be so limited.

There is a bias, in addition, in which paper and artifacts of the past were collected and preserved. Much of what has ended up in our historical societies and local archives has gotten there by chance—or by the idea that certain things are properly kept by a historical society. So the letters of a prominent family might be held in a local archive while the letters of a laborer in a tannery were not thought about or considered important enough to collect—or perhaps he didn't write or receive any letters. Most local historical societies have accepted whatever was offered them, and what was offered was usually given by people connected with the historical society or with prominent families in the community. Thus the diary of a workingwoman might not have made it into the local archive and was not, until recently, even sought. The same is true of materials generated by African Americans, whose letters, diaries, pictures, and newspapers are only rarely to be found in local archives. And when materials concerning African Americans, or Irish immigrants, or tenant farmers did appear in the collections in a society, those collections often were not indexed in a way to show their presence.

The caution we receive from Marc Bloch is somewhat different from Carl Becker's concerns. Bloch worried about our ability to understand the past. Be aware—not beware!—of the present, he said; be involved in your own times so that you will understand human nature, and knowing it in our time will aid in knowing it in the past. What he is warning us about is that too often the past is regarded as some golden age, and its inhabitants as giants of morality with clarity of action; whereas the past, in truth, was peopled by individuals whose motives were as varied as our own, whose actions were like ours. They need to be understood as human beings even when the documents fail to show them with their faults as well as their virtues. Knowing human nature today improves our understanding of the actions and motives of people in the past. Bloch cautions that the historian disinterested in his or her own era is most likely to become merely a useful antiquarian rather than a historian. This is something for us all to remember.

At this point you should be wondering whether we can do history at all. Or should we? With all these flaws in the documents, prejudices in ourselves and how we approach the past, in the topics we think are interesting, how can we even consider ourselves historians? Well, we can and we are. But we are better historians when we know our limitations, our interests, and our biases; when we think about the problem of materials that survive and those that do not; when we recognize that materials are as fragile in what they tell us as they are in their physical form—that they will not tell us everything; that we will have to approach them carefully, that we must seek out their biases as well as know our own, and that, in everything we do, there is a context that when sought will enrich our work.

Being aware is what is important. We can then research broadly, consider all the angles, approach a topic from various viewpoints, tease out the meanings in the materials that come to us from the past. These are the cautions a local historian—any historian, actually—must live with. Being aware of them, we will be sensitive to the fragility of what we do. Our communities deserve no less from us.

Despite the problems and pitfalls we are likely to encounter, we conduct local history research because it is important. Some of us are curious and want to know about the places where we live. Others seek answers to contemporary problems by looking at the past: why streets bear the names they do, why the town acquired a certain reputation, how the community reacted to national events, where the people came from—or where those who were once here went and why. Some use local history to understand how a community functioned—the town board reacts to certain strains placed on it by citizens' expectations, state requirements, or the lure of federal money. Some people want to research their own families or homes. Others want to know how a club, factory, or religious body came to be and then threaded its way through the years to the present. Some people, of course, are "professionals"—trained to be community, or public, historians—and they set out to conduct their working lives in one or various localities, interpreting the history of an institution or a place. There are many reasons to become involved. Thoughtful historians of our communities are always needed.

THERE ARE OTHERS WHO TEACH US

Now here is the update, and it is important, or at least has been to me. I have learned, as has the historical profession, that there is the past, and there is how we recall the past. Here I am indebted to my husband Michael Kammen (and isn't this an awkward bit as he needs no promotion by me) who has shown us in a raft of books that what happened and what we know about it is one historical problem, but another and equally important consideration is how we think about past events and how our thoughts have evolved over time. He, David Lowenthal, and John Bodnar have all written about memory: how Americans remember events, what events we forget, how we change our memories just as we change our clothing fashions and how over time some things sometimes become altered. This memory of place is something we all have, just as we have memories of events, even those we have not participated in: a past as told to us. Yet, our memories depend upon our own perspective, our little gray cells, as Hercule Poirot would say, and about how we have evolved over time—and have been influenced by the memories of others and the way that events have been recorded or talked about. I would not say that our memories are not our own, but that we are very influenced by backgrounds, viewpoints, contemporaries, environments, and what has been recorded as history about an event. Memory studies are not much engaged in by local historians but this perspective on the local gives us another way of seeing our hometowns and even our own lives and of charting change over time.

Other historians who have helped me to think about what history is include Susan Green and Laurel Thatcher Ulrich. Green is a historian of clothing, Ulrich has shown us the history in the object. The pursuit of genealogy—if not of my family but of the families of those I have researched—has opened up new and important pathways. Environmental historians have suggested new concerns revolving on physical change in a place, but also a sensory change over time. Do look at Joseph A. Amato's book *Rethinking Home: A Case for Writing Local History.*[5] A number of historians of the West have given me insight into thinking anew about topics that seem to be already well defined. I am also struck by those historians, including John Demos and William Cronen and Aaron Sachs, who understand the importance of writing well, of narrative, and of the historian's engagement with place. There are so many influences to consider and so many debts to pay.

NOTES

1. Spoken by the character Hugh O'Neil in the play *Making History* by Brian Friel (London: Faber and Faber, 1989), 8.

2. Carl Becker, *Everyman His Own Historian: Essays on History and Politics* (New York: S. F. Crofts, 1935; and in paper, Chicago: Quadrangle Paperbacks, 1966); Marc Bloch, *The Historian's Craft* (New York: Knopf, 1952) and *Ile-de-France: The Country around Paris* (Ithaca: Cornell University Press, 1971). See also the essays about local history in Carol Kammen, ed., *The Pursuit of Local History: Readings on Theory and Practice* (Walnut Creek, CA: AltaMira Press, 1996). In addition, see H. P. R. Finberg, ed., *Approaches to History* (London: Routledge and Kegan Paul, 1962), essays about history by a number of British historians.

3. See Carl Becker, *History of the Political Parties in the Province of New York, 1760–1776* (Madison: University of Wisconsin Press, 1909); and Marc Bloch, *Ile-de-France: The Country around Paris.*

4. Friel, *Making History*, 15–16.

5. Joseph A. Amato, *Rethinking Home: A Case for Writing Local History* (Berkeley: University of California Press, 2002).

Coda to Chapter 2

Censorship

There is a discernable community bias that local history should be promotional of place. It should add to the pleasure of living in that place, knowledge of place, and enjoyment. It should provide interesting stories to tell visitors and if it has, in its past, a robber, he becomes a folk hero, or a murderer, she too becomes a tale out of time rather than a blot on the record. All this also suits development and tourism directors and much of the public too and it provides fodder for articles in the local newspaper. Local history is thought to be nice and comforting and with this slant, assures an expectation of what should be known and broadcast.

Local historians also censor history. This self-censorship is important to recognize because it limits the topics that local historians select, it colors our outlook about the doing of local history for the communities in which we live, and it skews the sort of history that the local public expects and then gets from local historical societies and local historians.

What sort of censorship, you might ask? I offer here some anecdotal examples. A woman I knew told me that she would never look into the history of the failure of her local bank and the problems that caused the community because members of the family responsible were still living there. She did not want to disturb or embarrass them. In this case, she exercised local censorship in order to protect the living from an unpleasant past. In doing this, however, the historian was also denying the community an understanding of the role banks play in people's lives, how ordinary people reorder life when their savings disappear, and how a community acts to provide for those in great need. Would this historian, I wondered, be as careful to protect the owners of a failed supermarket who had relatively little social standing in the community or the owners of a railroad that abandoned the station, they being outside the community and relatively anonymous? The historian was willing to bypass an important local episode because it might cause people to think ill of prominent individuals. She surely could have handled this slice of local history without pointing fingers but, rather, by looking at the bank's importance to the community and the consequences of failure. What she worried about, I am sure, is that even if the man guilty of running off with the funds was before not named, people would still know, that they would remember on their own, that discussing the episode would "dredge it all up again."

Or was this historian protecting her ability to do local history locally? Local historians are dependent on the community for information and new materials. An "unreliable" local historian, one who embarrasses area residents or makes them uncomfortable, will soon find documents unavailable and people unwilling to cooperate. The public has certain expectations about local history, just as prominent people in the past often expected newspaper editors to protect the transgressions of their sons. "A local boy of good family," reads one newspaper notice in 1858, "fell into bad company when in town." The bad company was named, the son of the good family was not. To ignore local expectations can be a self-defeating scenario, for we must continue to live among those about whom, or for whom, we write.

Another form of local censorship involves what a historical society is willing to take on as an exhibit, program, or research topic. Some historical societies, conscious of the need for local support and contributions, are loath to touch subjects that might be seen as controversial. Local history, after all, is generally considered to be promotional of place. This censorship of presentation derives from the attitude that local history should be boosterish of— or be good for—the community. Our hometowns are avid consumers of local history because it is believed to have a positive influence on residents. In addition, local history helps provide tourist destinations—places such as cemeteries, record offices, and libraries that are visited and used by local and distant genealogists. Local history appears in the newspaper because it provides good "copy" or publicity about place.

A third variety of local censorship comes in the form of disappearing documents. A friend of mine, researching the lives of teenage girls in the nineteenth century, came across the record book of a home for unwed mothers. There was a good deal of information in the book about the young women, their ages, what happened to their babies, and where the mothers went from the home. On a second visit to consult this account, my friend was told that the book had been "lost." In that way, the keeper of the archive was able to censor what was studied and, consequently, what was known about the local past. Moreover, the "lost" document protected the community from the shame the archivist thought the information would place on it.

Local historians censor local history by limiting the topics investigated. There are some standard subjects that local history deals with, and there are other topics that are usually neglected, such as the study of local crime, race relations and racial conflict, the actions of strikers and bosses, the role of alcohol licensing, and political topics of all sorts, which are usually deemed as combative. These are legitimate subjects to pursue but are generally about divisive moments in our past; they do not promote a picture of a unified community consciousness and a harmonious past.

Another way in which local historians may censor the past is by a preference for beginnings rather than an examination of the development of a community over time or dealing with the decline of a town, a company, or a population. There is a bias for the remote past, for those first to till the land, early institutions, and how the community grew from a rude place to one of industry. A 106-page history of a city not far from my home devotes the first eighty pages to the period before the Civil War, relegating the 150 years since that time to a mere twenty pages. This surely represents a time warp in the way we perceive local history. It probably also reflects the fact that historical societies have not adequately collected the materials of the recent past. This cheats us of an opportunity to understand how the present came about and disguises the fact that we, ourselves, are living in historical times.

Historians also frequently ignore the history of technology. Yet the history of the sewing machine is important and interesting, for it eased the job of creating clothing and democratized fashion, as well. The history of the automobile allows us to see how residential patterns expanded, how an etiquette of the road developed, how advertising found a new venue, and how our language changed as well as our concept of time and space. The computer has also altered life in much the same way.[1]

Local historians, for a variety of reasons, have encountered censorship and have participated in it. We cannot always expand on the limitations that documents present us with, but by censoring our subjects, we shortchange our communities and ourselves. In presenting local history as always positive, we deny the fact that the past was as controversial and complicated as we know the present to be.

NOTE

1. Sharon Babian, "Technology and Local History," in Carol Kammen and Amy H. Wilson, eds., *Encyclopedia of Local History*, 2nd ed. (Lanham, MD: AltaMira Press, 2013).

Chapter Three

The Subjects of Local History

Parochial history . . . ought to consist of natural productions and occurrences as well as antiquities. . . . if stationary men would pay some attention to the districts on which they reside, they would publish their thoughts respecting the objects that surround them, from such materials might be drawn the most complete county histories, which are still wanting in several parts of this kingdom.

—Gilbert White, *The Natural History of Selborne* [1]

From the very start, local history in this country was about early settlers, the history of major institutions such as the first churches and schools, industries—especially those that produced a collectable product or drove the economy, fire companies, and railroads. These interests continued to be considered appropriate topics for local history, even as time went by. They followed closely the topics of early seventeenth-century local history in England—the history of royal and highborn families, church parishes and clergy, landownership and land division. These might be thought of as the established subjects of local history—the topics that made up the menu of what local historians traditionally researched and wrote about. There is nothing wrong with any of these individual subjects. The problem is that the scope of local history came to be restricted to these topics, even while there was so much more to consider. To be fair, the doing of history—both on the local level and when it became of some interest to the academy—has changed greatly over the past fifty years, as history in general has expanded to include previously neglected peoples and topics and as it has begun to explore new forms.

Even with the greater scope of late-twentieth-century history and that of the twenty-first century there are still many more topics that deserve our consideration. This leads us to ask, why the earlier restriction? The answer is that we must recall who was involved with local history and why. In many cases, local history was the preserve of the well established and well heeled: people with some stake in the community who led it in those days of deference to authority and wealth, who constituted its first families, and who established the community's first traditions. These early ways of thinking about local history hung on even in the face of social and demographic change, so that local history became the preserve of those of old stock, and the history collected and presented reflected that segment of the population. Others—African Americans, people of origins different from those who were first in a place, those who did not do well, or people who departed from a community, and women, of course—were, for the most part, left out of our local histories and probably would not, themselves, have expected to be included in the first place. They were generally too busy getting by, trying to succeed, or moving on to worry much about whose letters were being collected in the historical society or whose history was being told.

But history has come out of that closet, and today our local history belongs to all of us, immigrant and long established, those with ancestors buried in the local cemetery and the newly arrived. As Wallace Stegner has designated them, there are the rooted and the bare-root folks who are moved around from place to place. But even with new inclusions in historical interest, there are topics that are still generally avoided by local historical societies. And that in itself tells us some interesting things.

Few local historical societies or local historians dwell on divisiveness. They might produce narratives that are pleasing to read, but the histories that overlook conflict give the impression that people in the past lived more serene lives than we do. Local history is generally considered by most people to be a way of building community; a way to "boom" the town, to promote its history, and to bring people together into a common past; or a way to understand place. That does explain why the history of local politics is rarely a topic of local history, for politics, by its very nature, is competitive. Yet what is more vital and important to a community than its politics?

What about those people who leave a town? They are most often forgotten, unless, of course, they name their next hometown for the place from which they just departed or return with wealth or interesting experiences to share. Otherwise, out-migration is rarely looked at in a critical way. Yet those who leave do so because of some siren call from elsewhere or because of a push from their starting place: a lack of jobs for young men or a lack of land might be considered sufficient reasons to feel pushed from one's home place. The pull of land elsewhere has always been potent, as has the possibility of employment. Local historians study the institutions of a community: the churches, schools, and industries. We are happy to focus on that which has prospered, what a place is known for, how a town or village grew, what spurred it on. It is easy to forget about the industries or ideas that failed, the lives disrupted that cast community members out of work and also depressed the local economy and outlook causing, in many instances, a departure from place.

Because local history is perceived to be vital to community building, topics that are disruptive are often ignored. Few local historians consider strikes or economic downturns, those who lease rather than own land, or those who make their living, legally or not, by selling alcohol. We are unlikely to find much in written local history about lawlessness, unless it is picturesque and produced a criminal-hero. In my community we have Edward Rulloff, who murdered his wife and child, hiding them in a trunk that he tossed into our deep lake. He probably also killed several others. Today, he is recalled as a great scoundrel rather than as a cold-blooded killer, and there is even a local restaurant named for him, though very few people recall who Edward Rulloff really was. This is the Jesse James syndrome, but there was really nothing romantic about some of these bad guys (and gals).

Nor have local historians adequately explored the influence of changing technology on communities: What happened when street lighting became possible? Where were the lights put? Who was on the electrical circuit? Who was served by the new water-treatment plant? Where did rubbish go, and how, over time, has the collection of trash changed? What happened as the result of airport placement? What were the debates about the route of a new road or turnpike or landfill? What happens when newspapers fade or fail? These topics are all too infrequently explored. Perhaps now that we are settling comfortably into the twenty-first century, topics such as these from the twentieth will take on new appeal.

Local historical societies and local historians have begun to delve into some of the questions raised by the twentieth century. There are a great many topics that might be considered, although there is a perceptual problem in that so much of twentieth-century history looks as if, or is regarded as if, it is national rather than local history. It can, however, be both. Following are some suggestions for twentieth-century topics:

- If World War II is a national topic because most decisions were made outside our hometowns, the issue of who became the officers of the local selection board and how that board functioned is a local topic. Who went to war, how did their families fare, what did women do for the war effort—what about those who did not themselves participate in the military or resisted service?
- If the passage of the Nineteenth Amendment is a national question, how local men and women reacted to the long fight for suffrage is certainly a local topic. Who was for suffrage, and what were the common traits that bound them? Who was against it, and how did they express their displeasure? Was the local fight fought on the same grounds as the national battle?

Was leadership local, or did it come from outside the community? What was the effect on the politics of the place with new voters on the voter rolls after 1920? What needs to be explored is why men, who were the voters before 1920, decided to vote in the affirmative. Were they advancing their wives or protecting their daughters?

- The abortion debate is a national issue; it is also local and it is decidedly uncomfortable. Sides have been taken, marches organized, signs carried, and in some sad instances, shots have rung out. Who supported choice? Where did the leadership come from: in my community, our representative in Albany in the 1970s was Republican Constance E. Cook, a staunch supporter of safe and legal medical abortions and who crafted legislation that became a model for the Supreme Court decision in 1973. Locally, it was the minister of the Baptist church, David Evans, who saw to it that women had the funds and means for safe abortions. What is the story in your community?

- Race is probably the most difficult topic we have to deal with in this country. How have questions of race played out locally? Were African Americans mentioned in the nineteenth-century newspaper? Were there racist cartoons to be found? What housing patterns pertained? Were there business opportunities for black adults or did they need to leave for elsewhere to find employment? Was a community redlined in terms of bank loans for homes? Were there places the races mingled? In the twentieth century, did the Depression touch blacks and whites in the same way, and were both aided equally by state and federal programs? What were the issues the races battled over or didn't discuss at all, and what were the issues that brought them together? What about employment opportunities for blacks and how did people in a locality react to the searing times during the Civil Rights era? How has black history—or the history of American Indians or people of different ethnic groups—become part of the local story?

- Consumerism has created a new society: What about it can be documented locally? What new products are available? What are the items in demand? Is there a local style? Have easily obtainable products or stores changed the look of our communities? Consider how Halloween has become a major holiday with ubiquitous lawn ornaments—those Styrofoam ghosts and cemetery stones, those giant spiderwebs—where once, some time ago, things, including costumes, were mostly homemade. What about the local mall? When did it develop, and how quickly did it displace Main Street? Or, perhaps the community fought back, and it didn't. That is an important local story.

- Culinary changes tell us a good deal about a community over time. Can we define the local ways in which a place participates in culinary trends or sets its own? Farmers' markets have become popular, along with environmentalism and localism. This is important to document. How would you document these topics in your hometown?

- Home styles have changed. The architecture of our houses is different today and how homes are advertised has also changed. Today, kitchens and bathrooms are featured; once it was the number of bedrooms or the school district. These changes reflect our times and values.

In an essay by Paul Leuilliot entitled "The Defense and Illustration of Local History," reprinted in *The Pursuit of Local History*, this French historian sets out several principles that he believes suggest the underlying nature of local history.[2] These present interesting avenues of pursuit. The first principle is that local economic history in the nineteenth century leads into the present and illuminates our present-day preoccupations. Marc Bloch, he recalls, suggested that local history, by definition, is rooted in a specific bit of territory but can move from the present back to the past and that it is important to trace agrarian history, population changes, financial history, and the history of technology. This does not mean, however, that there is a straight line between the past and the present, for there were many twists and turns from then to now. The past did not determine the present as much as provide a base from which things current sprang—some with clean connections, others with bumps and twists and turns along the way so that there could have been no telling then what would grow from that time to ours.

The second principle is that local history is better suited for qualitative studies than quantitative ones. Leuilliot believes this because accurate figures, for agriculture, for example, are hard to obtain (although he was speaking mostly about France; our census figures describe agricultural output). There are, however, a number of quantitative studies that can be conducted at the local level. I am thinking in particular about studies of voting patterns, of the disbursal of land or of its concentration especially as family farms disappear into housing developments or giant corporate agribusiness, of the rise and fall in the population of an area, of family size, and of certain agricultural products, especially those that were tracked in federal and state census figures and were imported or exported from the home place.

Leuilliot's third principle is that local history requires a "certain flexibility, for it is a loosely knit history."[3] His point is that local history usually cannot offer long runs of statistical material on any one subject. This is a bit perplexing, for in French departments and parishes there are very long runs of vital statistics; in this country, though it is younger than France, there are also statistics to which we can turn. We are able to construct interesting historical questions to be answered by using the federal and state censuses to look at the ethnic diversity of the population over time. In many places we can look at voting patterns, political party affiliation, and the growth of population density. On the other hand, Leuilliot believes that local history is the place to study structures over time. He suggests that industries, such as a vineyard—good Frenchman that he is—can reveal the ways in which that business was run in order to make a profit.

Leuilliot calls for local history to relate to daily life. The very best proponent of this is a lovely book by Françoise Zonabend called *Enduring Memory: Time and History in a French Village*, a detailed study of daily and seasonal life that investigates much that we take for granted and rarely bother to document at all.[4] This study, one that brings together history and anthropology, is one that local historians should pay special attention to as a model of what might be done with local documents and traditions. It is also chockfull of interesting topics that easily translate from the French scene to the American experience.

Leuilliot observes that local history provides a place to look at the history of things that cannot be seen, such as bravery, or pride, or contraceptive practices, or thrift; it is the history of things that are given, that do not have to be talked about—though so much the better if they are—such as money and its less visible confrere, thrift, and it is the history of the durable, of things that last over the years, of age-old traditions, or folklore, if you prefer to call it that. Here local history overflows into the history of mentalities, of attitudes toward life, death, money, and innovation.[5]

Leuilliot calls for local history to be differential, by which he means that we look at the disparity between national or regional events and those same situations at home. The history of the automobile fits into this pattern and can be studied as a part of our national history, but we can also look at the automobile in a locality and use one aspect of this history to illuminate the other. Think of the ways that places changed after the appearance of the auto: roads were improved, an etiquette developed that soon became law; time and distance changed in our speech patterns; encounters between car and horse were signs of transition as were the disappearance of wagon shops as car repair and gasoline stations emerged. All this can be tracked in local newspapers, in pictures of the era, and in court records.

There is probably no subject more troublesome to American local historians than the Underground Railroad, another national story that has very particular local outcomes. Conceived in secrecy, conducted in silence, the passage of African Americans north left few records to tell its story—and far too many places said to be associated with it. Sources are the main problem—the lack of them and the responsible use of those that do exist. "I had a diary giving the names, dates, and circumstances of all the slaves I had helped run away," wrote John Parker, an escaped slave and thereafter an aide to runaways who traveled through Ripley, Ohio. An account of Parker's life appears in *His Promised Land*, edited by Stuart Seeley Sprague. Parker explains that as a family man, a property owner, and the proprietor of a business, he had a great deal to lose if his record book were discovered. So "as a matter of safety," he wrote, "I threw this diary into the iron furnace, for fear it might fall into other hands." This caution was shared. Parker explains that after passage of the Fugitive Slave Act in 1850, "everyone engaged in the work destroyed all existing evidence of his connection with it." The work of aiding fugitives, however, continued apace. "In fact," he writes, it was "more aggressively than ever [pursued], which speaks well for the conscience and courage" of those involved.[6]

Under the circumstances, it is easy to see that the sources for the study of the Underground Railroad are difficult to come by and why those that have survived are especially to be treasured. It is also easy to understand why local enthusiasts, eager to find evidence of abolition activity, have expanded on those sources using local folklore and historical fiction, willing to suspend critical analysis at the very time when we need to take the most care. Yet, precisely because reliable information is scarce, the local historian of the Underground Railroad needs to be even more vigilant regarding the subject. A casual collection of the oral and the supposed, the romantic and the impossible, brings doubt down around the entire topic—which is exactly the opposite of the desired result.

About no other local topic, except possibly the weather, are there more legends, more hearsay, more dubious claims, or more details to question. Yet footnotes, when they appear, tend to recite earlier works that contained no notes—sources that are dubious at best. In a field in which much information has been gathered orally, it is important that the reason be given why an informant deserves to be believed. In one article on the Underground Railroad, the author cites an undocumented and untrustworthy church history, a pamphlet written without footnotes, and repeats stories heard from a variety of people, not all of whom are credible and one who was called the "local liar." There was, however, nothing in the source notes to differentiate among them.

Throughout upstate New York there is no topic concerning freedom seekers more hotly debated than that of tunnels. There was once a tunnel, "they say," from a local temperance tavern to the lakeshore, a distance of at least a mile, through which escaped slaves were supposed to move on their way to a boat ride farther north. The terrain in this part of the state, where this legend was collected, is glacial deposit—sometimes ten inches or less of soil resting upon shale. The critical mind notes that today when the New York State Department of Transportation improves a local road it brings in an assortment of yellow work trucks that include dozers and bucket loaders and jackhammers, and sometimes it even resorts to the use of dynamite to blast through the rock. If that is what happens today in order to dig out side ditches and improve the roadbed or to create a new road altogether, then it seems logical to conclude that in the 1850s a farmer with nothing but a shovel and ax is unlikely to have dug a mile-long tunnel for escaping slaves who might or might not come along to use it. The time and labor alone should cause us to doubt. Nonetheless, tunnel myths abound! A disbelief in tunneling does not diminish the fact that there was Underground Railroad activity in the area. To separate fact from fiction is the historian's job, and it can be done knowing full well that genuine accounts present us thrilling stories needing no embellishment.

There are good sources, of course, in addition to Parker's diary or the notes published by William Still and others. From Troy, New York, there are particularly helpful and illuminating references in a local newspaper in which the Vigilant Committee reported that fifty-seven persons had passed through their care in the previous year at a cost to the society of $125.40. The federal census also provides important information: look at the birthplaces of African Americans in 1850. About fifty of the 141 adult African Americans in my county were born in the South, leading me to believe that most had come from slavery. On the other hand, the federal census can also substantiate the mobility of the black community and the fear engendered by the passage of the Fugitive Slave Act, for fewer than six of the fifty were still in my community in 1860.

Who helped those fleeing north? In Ithaca there was a lawyer named Ben Johnson. A local historian reporting on Johnson's efforts to aid escaping slaves wrote that Johnson would claim he was a Christian, and a lawyer, and a Democrat, and therefore a law-abiding citizen, meaning that, as such, he could not assist in depriving men of their property because he was an officer of the court and sworn to uphold its laws. But, as the local historian explains, Johnson's words of self-definition would be accompanied by him handing over five or ten dollars, directing the agent to "take it and buy tickets, and send the runaway slaves back to their masters." He knew, and others knew, that the money for tickets would be used to send runaways farther on their way "toward the North Star." Thus, saying one thing and meaning another was Johnson's way of abiding by the law and breaking it at the same time.[7]

That there was abolition activity on behalf of fugitives is something on which we can all agree. The extent of the aid is another thing altogether, and it demands that we be cautious. We know that some fugitives came through the area. But we do not know much about the extent to which they were feared, resented, or even reported to the authorities. Especially important to remember is that those who aided fugitives frequently did so in a climate of local hostility.

John Parker noted that in Ripley, Ohio, there was considerable Underground Railroad activity, yet "the town itself was proslavery as well as the country around it." Antagonism, in the form of attacks against those involved in underground activity or in a lack of willingness to aid or to participate, is very much a part of the story to be told.

An important question to ask is: why should so much interest in Underground Railroad history erupt at the end of the twentieth century? There are many possible answers. By century's end the generation that fought World War II had aged, and those people began to tell their own stories. The book *Lest Innocent Blood Be Shed: The Story of the Village of LeCambon and How Goodness Happened* encouraged thought about those who helped the Jews escape.[8] Anne Frank's diary, the book and movie *Schindler's List* (1993), and other works, fictive and real, have created great interest in and sympathy for those who risked their lives to aid the Jews of Europe a half century ago. The Underground Railroad provides an American counterpart to that activity and to the moral choices posed a century earlier. The Sanctuary Movement of the 1980s, in which some Americans gave aid and shelter to Central Americans who fled to this country, might also have spurred interest in the historical activity. Biographies and fictional accounts of the life of Harriet Tubman have also exploded in number and may be another reason for the popularity of this subject, as flight is exciting and pursuit creates tension in stories. There are probably more books about Harriet Tubman for children these days than stories about George Washington.

Recent popular fiction has addressed the topic too. There is David Bradley's complex novel, *The Chaneysville Incident*, and Miriam Grace Monfredo's *North Star Conspiracy*, in which her Seneca Falls librarian-detective Glynis Tryon solves a mystery that originated with escaping fugitives from the South. The Underground Railroad has long been a subject of interest to novelists. *Fire Bell in the Night* by Constance Robertson is one of the earliest books of this genre.[9]

In addition, Underground Railroad activities have been featured on television shows, and the topic is an active destination on the Internet. There was a well-publicized walk along a supposed route and postings online about this journey. In Buffalo there is an Underground Railroad tour one can take complete with period clothing and the fear of being chased. And, of course, there is a new museum devoted to the experience of those escaping slavery in Cincinnati, Ohio. Newspapers, too, have cited Underground Railroad sites as tourist attractions, communities have publicized them on historic markers, and historical websites eagerly make connections to this activity. Most important, local historians have turned to the subject in their search for understanding and illumination of African American local history, which until recently had been long neglected and is still difficult to research.

These are symptoms of current interest in the subject. The most overriding reason for a revival of interest in the history of Underground Railroad activity is surely that in this nation, where race has been identified as among our most pressing national concerns, tales of the Underground Railroad soothe misgivings about the nature of that conflict. They stress interracial cooperation, giving some people a way of asserting moral correctness about the position they think they would have taken—or that their communities did take. This is because actions of those involved in the Underground Railroad rested on what we see today as clear moral choices; it is easy for us to reduce the whole issue to right and wrong. In truth, it was much more complicated. Underground Railroad activity becomes a symbol of positive behavior in our long national anguish over race. Abolition and Underground Railroad activity help us prove to ourselves that all white people were not guilty of racism, that blacks, whites, and Native Americans did take actions we can look on as moral when they gave succor to the fugitive escaping an unjust situation. These earlier positions echo through the ages the message that racial cooperation is possible.

But desiring to claim the moral high road and finding evidence to do so are two very different things. And while the public is often willing to suspend critical thinking regarding the Underground Railroad, and while local publicists and local color writers tout cultural tourism and actively incorporate every shred of evidence or hearsay into the local story, it is clearly incumbent upon the local historian to proceed with caution.

And this is exactly what I have found local historians are doing. In the face of a general disregard of the facts on the part of teachers, journalists, and others, joined with a desire to find links that make a community, or group, or individual look good on this topic, it is the local historians who are saying, "Wait! Let's look at what the facts really tell us, what we can honestly assert." The problem, however, is that schoolteachers in particular and others in general are so eager for any information that they hastily incorporate whatever is available without distinguishing between that which might be credible and that which is not, that which can be proved and that which is clearly fanciful.

This does not mean that we should abandon interest in or research about the story of the Underground Railroad. It does mean that fact needs to be separated from folklore—not every root cellar was a hidey-hole or evidence of abolitionist activity and not every Quaker household aided fugitives, although many did—that we must judge the evidence carefully and put the story of the Underground Railroad into its community context. This means we must admit that locally there were many people—often the majority of the population, as Parker suggests—who were unwilling to aid fugitives and even anxious to turn them, and those helping them, over to the authorities.

The story of the Underground Railroad is more complicated and more interesting than simply one of escaped slaves and those who aided their progress north. The story is really the story of community conflict, of moral decision making, of the law-abiding—who did not aid fugitives, even if they might have wanted to—and of those courageous people who took risks in order to lend a needed hand. The story is also of communities known as safe and those that were decidedly unsafe. It is the story of a shifting network of ways out of the South that changed with time and local attitudes, one particular route used on one day, a different way used on another. It is the story of churches that split apart over this issue and of ministers finding ways to justify the return of slaves because they were under the aegis of the laws of Caesar, not the laws of God. It is also the story of individual courage, for not all slaves ran, not all who ran kept going, and not all those who kept going made it out.

All of this makes the Underground Railroad even more interesting and important because in context it becomes evidence of courage and moral character. It is and will remain a story of helpers who willingly risked their own safety to aid those in need, and most importantly, it is the story of the slaves themselves—some well known like Frederick Douglass or Harriet Tubman, but most not—who dared to escape.

We need to relate what is verifiable within a local context. We need to stress the ad hoc, unsystematic nature of the passage of fugitives from the South. We need to acknowledge the risky nature of giving aid and the unwillingness of some good people to do so. And we need to celebrate the genuine heroes of the era. John P. Parker of Ripley, Ohio, was certainly one of them. But so, too, are the local historians today who are being careful with the work that they do concerning this subject and are true to what they can document.

If the history of abolition is difficult because of a lack of documents, there are other previously neglected subjects for which there is a great deal of material: architectural history, changes in the environment, agricultural innovation, educational history, the history of local communities as they change to serve the greater public demands. These topics all come with ample documentation, as does even the history of what we eat.

In newspapers, tucked into books, jotted in journals, and written in diaries or at the back of account books, Americans—especially women—recorded recipes. I have read the directions for making worm tea to cure the ailing, mixtures to take out stains, and cake recipes like this one for Jell Cake, dated 1869:

  2 cups sugar
  3/4 cup butter
  2 cups flour
  3 eggs
  2 tsps. cream of tartar
  1 nutmeg
  2 teaspoons of soda dissolved in a cup of sweet milk [10]

Our recipes today come with a few more directions, but we, too, pass them along on small cards, include them in letters, tear them from newspapers, and even file them on our computers. But: where did that nutmeg come from and how did it get to the community? It certainly didn't grow here, and its story takes us back to European desire for control over goods produced elsewhere and of European deals in which land was traded from one country to another.

The historical material includes directions for making cakes and pies, jams and jellies, cookies and vegetable dishes; suggestions for tonics and "physicks"; and any number of cleaning solutions sure to remove dirt and stains. And there is no better place to look for information about the household than in our home communities. Household and culinary information tell us about ourselves as individuals, as members of families, of ethnic groups, and of geographic communities with specific traditions. Culinary taboos and preferences play out in the locality: the appearance of vegetarian restaurants and a boycott of certain foods on the basis of politics or morality are significant local events. The history of lettuce is a case in point: iceberg lettuce was developed because it was easy to ship and so became ubiquitous, but it also became the symbol of a fight for fairness for the mostly Hispanic farm workers who cut the lettuce in the fields and so there were boycotts against buying it. Today, the preferred salad greens (another change of language that tells us something) are those produced locally.

Culinary history is also an excellent place to observe the advance of technology. Recipes preserve past foodways, while they also provide information about the production of local foodstuffs and their uses and the introduction of new foods. They illuminate cooking techniques now long abandoned. They also tell much about the technology of the kitchen—technology that has consistently transformed work in the home and linked home to market.

When I think of my recipes, they fall neatly into two categories: those before I acquired a Cuisinart and those after 1977. My food processor allows me to make a variety of dishes I had not cooked before or had cooked once and decided they were too time-consuming or bothersome to prepare again. This same "revolution" occurred for women who gave up the open hearth for a cookstove and for those who moved from cooking with wood to gas or electric stoves and ovens. The microwave has further revolutionized kitchen capabilities while creating new habits and possibilities. Consider this new means of food preparation and the foods that have been created specifically for it. Consider, too, the microwave in terms of what it has meant for women who work outside the home.

Not only do recipes reflect information about ingredients and techniques, about families and individuals, they also testify to regional specialties— about things that draw people together in patterns of identification with place. I think immediately of Buffalo wings, New England chowder, beignets of New Orleans, blue corn piki bread at the Hopi's Second Mesa, Wallapa Bay oysters, South Carolina hickory smoked pork, ambrosia (that green Jell-O studded with marshmallows found everywhere in Iowa), *spiedes* of Binghamton, New York, and *fasnachts* in Ephrata, Pennsylvania. And of course, the many varieties of barbeque sauce. These, and many others, are foods that depend on and celebrate local produce. Though eaten elsewhere, they are linked specifically to place, and they enhance the definition of place.

The sources for this rich culinary history exist in our archives, like preserves on a shelf, awaiting our interest. They tantalize but also puzzle us. Some are difficult to understand because the terms used mean little to us today: the ingredients are unfamiliar, the techniques unusual. Some of the recipes are difficult for us because we are accustomed to precision of measurement, whereas many of those older recipes call for a pinch of cloves or a handful of flour or "some butter."

Most of us would have little interest in actually cooking and serving many of those old recipes because they reflect a different era or dated thinking about what is healthy or fashionable. An article a few years ago in the *New York Times* published just before Thanksgiving noted, "An amble through the old recipe file is a walk down a most unhealthy memory lane. There's Mother's turkey stuffing, rich enough to clog several arteries; her sugar rich cranberry mold in its base of Jell-O; the casserole featuring Velveeta cheese." My aunt's collection of family recipes directs me to use one dozen eggs in her sand cake and nothing but butter, and lots of it, in Christmas cookies. She also calls for rosewater and glycerin. The last two ingredients I can purchase from my druggist, though I am unlikely to do so, the butter I forgo, and there is no way these days that I would put one dozen eggs into anything. Her recipes, however, also testify to her ethnicity and my own.

While we might not want to serve these dishes today, those recipes of fifteen, or fifty, or one hundred fifty years ago tell us about food preferences of another time, about food fads, culinary influences, and health considerations. They reveal the culture of our cuisine. Times change, health concerns change, and our culinary habits follow.

Our relatively new historical interest in food mirrors our contemporary obsession with food. Look at the shelves of any bookstore and count the number of new cookbooks. Look at the magazines devoted to cooking. Think, too, about the current popularity of the personal memoir, in which food and food habits often reflect the stability (and idiosyncrasies) of family life.

There is a growing academic interest in food and food history. *Food and Foodways* is an international journal devoted to the history and culture of food. *Food History News* also relates culinary history, mostly that of North America. And on the Internet there are thousands of links that appear when one requests items about food and history.

Sandra Oliver, who edits *Food History News* from her home in Maine, is also the author of a book that is a perfect blend—or roux (a mix of flour, butter, and heat), if you will—of food, history, and place. The book, published by Connecticut's Mystic Seaport Museum, is called *Saltwater Food-ways.*[11] Oliver, who practiced open-hearth cooking for some years, has studied the area's foodways and related them to specific physical sites open to the public at Mystic Seaport. She carefully discusses the food that would have been cooked in a seaman's cottage, foods and their preparation in the home of a merchant family, foods available, technological changes in the kitchen, and storage of food in a more affluent home. She also looks at the food served on whaling ships that put out from Connecticut harbors and at the ingredients that might have been encountered in foreign ports, the food offered and the role of a cook on fishing vessels, and the foodways of those who made their livelihood working in a local lighthouse.

Oliver touches on the etiquette of food in different settings, storage problems and solutions, different cooking techniques, the changing cast of characters who actually prepared meals, and the cultural implications of meals eaten together and those "taken on the run." This book, which looks at the foodways of people along the southern Connecticut shore, is an important beginning for an understanding of North American foodways. It can only be hoped that Oliver's broad research plan, beginning with architectural evidence and ranging widely through library and archival records, will be followed and adapted by others to develop information and discussion of the foodways of other parts of the country.

Now is the time for researchers to dig out the recipes and directions buried in letters and diaries to help define the foods that Americans ate, learn about the introduction of "foreign" ingredients and techniques, and look at the relationship of farm to market and how that expanded because of transportation technology. We should begin by defining the terms used, the foods eaten, and the various methods of preparation in order to understand our culinary history and appreciate that which has continued from one generation to another and that which has changed.

In addition—and this will hardly prove unpleasant—we should document the foodways of our own time by collecting information about those little places that prepare local specialties and the roadside stands and regional festivals that feature foods that define an area. In this, Jane and Michael Stern have pioneered. See their *Roadfood* and *Goodfood* for starters.[12] There are some tasty dishes to sample and much to learn when we look up and cook up the recipes in our local archives. Bon appétit!

For some time now, I have kept a list of topics that local historians rarely tackle. There are many reasons why particular historical subjects have been ignored. In some cases it is because the topic has not been seen as important or community building, which is what many regard to be the purpose of local history. In other cases the sources for a particular study are scarce or difficult to use; some subjects require skills local historians do not have or do not care to learn—mathematics, for example, or accounting, or a foreign language. In some cases, the subjects have simply not dawned on those of us who do local history—their time has not yet come—or they do not interest us personally.

In some cases, historians have tackled these topics, so I do not want to imply that they have all been totally ignored. But I find these subjects all too infrequently treated in exhibits, discussions, and even local historical society pamphlets. And I wonder why. See what you think:

- In reading nineteenth-century newspapers I have been struck by the frequency with which the excise laws are mentioned. Excise? Well, I looked up the word, remembering it only vaguely from a long-ago college history course. Excise is the duty levied on the manufacture, sale, or consumption of commodities within the country. It is the opposite of import duties. Excise is not something I get very excited about these days, but then, I don't own a sports team needing a license or run a company whose products are regulated, such as tobacco.

In the context of nineteenth-century local history, however, excise laws meant, among other things, the taxation and regulation of alcohol: who could sell beer, liquor, and wine; when; to whom; and under what conditions. Excise laws also meant revenue from licenses sold and taxes collected. Who got those licenses in a locality is important to know because permits often followed political power and were limited in number. How saloons, inns, and hotels sold alcohol was a matter of local concern, especially after the rise of the temperance movement.

So excise laws are important. They can tell us a great deal about how a community worked, about local concerns and needs—for revenue and for the regulation of alcohol—and also about local political power. All this was, of course, before the advent of Prohibition, when the story changes and becomes even more interesting.

- This leads to another neglected topic. Rarely are there local studies or exhibits about community politics. Now, I know that often there are displays of political memorabilia—campaign buttons and posters, for example. And there are also talks and discussions about significant political shifts such as in 1856, when the Republican Party made its appearance, or in the 1928 presidential campaign when Al Smith ran and ruffled the prohibitionists' feathers. But long-term political studies by local historians are few. The reason for this is surely that politics is viewed as divisive; it represents a rift in the community.[13] Yet we have neglected an important aspect of our community life by not looking seriously at local politics. Consider the amount of space given to politics in old newspapers—in fact, in many others, local newspapers were organs of different political parties or viewpoints. Consider the amount of time and energy spent on local issues and then, every two or four years, on national issues reflected through a local lens. How often has local political history been researched?

- Strikes are another topic more often neglected than addressed. Of course, certain major strikes are known, such as the Homestead Strike of 1892, the Pullman Strike of 1894, and the coal strike of 1902. But rarely considered are the attempts by labor to organize and improve conditions locally, prodded into being either by local factory conditions or by outside forces. Unions represent important efforts on the part of working people to better their conditions—to raise pay, lessen hours, make the workplace safe— and have organized representation in negotiations with factory owners. Yet the history of union formation or local strikes is rarely looked at by local historical agencies, possibly because the owners of factories were more likely to support a historical organization than was labor. As we expand our idea of who is a proper research target, the people on the picket line should be part of the picture.

- Another aspect of labor history is the role of children and youth. Few local studies look at indentured servants, many of whom were children. Child labor is more often researched and written about in a national setting than on the local level. What were the working conditions for children? Who worked, and how did that work change over the course of the past two centuries? Where did child workers come from, and how was their labor used and regulated? In my community, most child labor was probably to be found on the farm, and many of the children were from farm families or local orphans turned over to farm families—their labor in exchange for food, clothing, and sometimes schooling. But there were also children involved in the cigar industry and other factory work, and we have few local studies of this important issue. In addition, who accepted indentured servitude, how long did it last, and what were the conditions required when the time expired?

- Debt is another neglected subject. Certainly debt is an important facet of business life, especially in the life of farmers. It raises the question of the role of banks in our communities. How have people addressed the need for new capital, how has debt been managed, and what have been the consequences of failure—of a farm or of a factory? Failure is a topic that enlarges, its consequences expanding outward rather like the ripples from a small stone dropped in water. What happens when a bank fails? What happens when a major company relocates? Most recently, what happens when mortgages cannot be met and houses become property of banks, thereby undermining local home prices? These are issues to look at in the past, and they can be studied today as well. A local study of how workers coped with the loss of livelihood would be an important contribution to a community's self-knowledge: Where did those workers go for aid? To whom did they turn? Where did those workers find other work? Did they stay in the town, shifting to another factory; did they set out on their own; or did they leave so that the failure also caused a loss of local labor—and population?

- Equally neglected is the subject of crime. Most historical societies know and discuss dramatic murder cases. Few local historians or local historical agencies, however, have taken a close look at a docket book of a local judge or court to see what sorts of cases came to trial, how they were disposed of, who became embroiled with the law, and how the legal system served the community.

This is a very partial list of topics infrequently pursued by the local historian. There are a great many other subjects that need to be addressed. In fact, there are too many interesting and important topics for any one lifetime. As my coffee mug reminds me each morning: so many topics, so little time.

NOTES

1. Gilbert White, *The Natural History of Selborne* (New York: Harper and Brothers [n.d.]; reprint of 1788 edition).
2. Paul Leuilliot, "The Defense and Illustration of Local History," in *The Pursuit of Local History*, ed. Carol Kammen (Walnut Creek, CA: AltaMira Press, 1996), 164–80.
3. Leuilliot, "The Defense and Illustration of Local History," 169.
4. Françoise Zonabend, *Enduring Memory: Time and History in a French Village*, trans. Anthony Forster (Manchester: Manchester University Press, 1984).
5. Leuilliot, "The Defense and Illustration of Local History," 171.
6. Stuart Seeley Sprague, ed., *His Promised Land: The Autobiography of John P. Parker, Former Slave and Conductor on the Underground Railroad* (New York: Norton, 1996).
7. This story is recounted in Thomas Burns, *Initial Ithacans Comprising Sketches and Portraits of the Forty-four Presidents of the Village of Ithaca* (Ithaca: Journal Press, 1904), 13–15.
8. See Philip P. Hallie, *Lest Innocent Blood Be Shed: The Story of the Village of LeCambon and How Goodness Happened* (New York: Harper, 1994).
9. David Bradley, *The Chaneysville Incident* (New York: Harper and Row, 1981); Miriam Grace Monfredo, *North Star Conspiracy* (New York: St. Martin's Press, 1993). Constance Robertson, *Fire Bell in the Night* (Philadelphia: Blakiston Co., 1944).
10. This recipe is from the 1869 diary of Carrie Manning, DeWitt Historical Society, Ithaca.
11. Sandra Oliver, *Saltwater Foodways: New Englanders and Their Food, at Sea and Ashore, in the Nineteenth Century* (Mystic, CT: Mystic Seaport Museum, 1995).
12. Jane Stern and Michael Stern, *Roadfood and Goodfood* (New York: Knopf, 1986).
13. Rita Smidt's, *Lansing at the Crossroads: A Partisan History of the Village of Lansing, New York* (San Jose: Writers Club Press, 2001) is an interesting exception to this. Smidt was a participant when the Village of Lansing separated itself from the Town of Lansing; her book recounts that episode. Not everyone agrees with her position or her recollection of events, but the book is a valuable account of a time many people regard as "relatively painful."

Coda to Chapter 3

Journalists and Historians

All too familiar to local historians is the telephone call from a friendly journalist: a newspaper reporter, feature writer, or someone from the local television studio. "What do you know about the person being honored by the street renaming this morning?" the journalist will ask. Or, when did the railroad come through? When was that church built? Who founded that business? Can you give me a quick history of the local Y? Or, what can you tell me about the Underground Railroad (especially during Black History month)? Or, what local women do we have of note (during March, Women's History week)? What about the celebration of the Fourth of July in the past (you know when), or, about tragedies in the local lake/river/sea (usually in the summer), or about the earthquake of 1859, the tornado of 1936, the flood of 1972? What about Indian villages once located here, battles fought nearby; the first local schools; the community center and how it was used during the Depression? How did they celebrate Thanksgiving one hundred years ago or the ways that Christmas became commercialized—and when?

Sigh. Some of this we know. A good deal we don't know—or we don't know well enough to be comfortable giving responses off the cuff, offhand, and without looking up the exact dates, the previous owners, the number of dead, the make of the car. We need to be sure about the information we pass along. We are people who like to be as accurate as possible.

But because we are good-hearted, because sometimes the question is really interesting, because we understand the broad impact of the media, because we want reporters and others "to get the story right," we hasten to our notes, our books, and our files. We rustle about like squirrels looking for acorns buried the past autumn that must be just over here, or there, and if at all possible we get the needed information. That is what local historians do.

These examples highlight some of the differences between historians and journalists. As local historians we are dedicated to getting the facts right, understanding events in context, and looking for the complexities that answers to direct questions sometimes contain. We plod a bit and are cautious about how we make statements because we understand the power of the press—a power that we respect. In addition, we know that once something appears in print, it easily passes into local knowledge as gospel and is likely to be picked up and reused the next time the subject comes up. "Well, I saw it in the newspaper," is a comment I frequently hear. We recognize the power of the printed word, so we try hard to be accountable. And to be truthful, we are glad we were asked rather than the journalist making a stab at finding the information and not getting it right, or only getting half the story, or being satisfied with someone's rendition, which might or might not be true.

Journalists, on the other hand, have other priorities. Journalists work with pressing deadlines, they serve demanding editors who want stories "now," and they are driven by space constraints that force them to be succinct—to boil the story down. They need answers, not qualifications, and adjustments, contingencies and explanations. They need, most of all, to get the story, and they like getting it right. But beyond getting the facts right, journalists can make do with getting information attributed to someone else—something historians cannot do or be satisfied with in the same way.

Take old Mr. Tompkins. If he tells a journalist what he believes happened at that old place on the corner during Prohibition, or about the time when those two fellas got stuck up that tree, or about crop disasters one particular year, his information can appear in the newspaper the following day as what Mr. Tompkins said, or observed, or even what he believed to be true. If Mr. Tompkins tells his stories to a historian, we follow a different route, one that includes consideration of context, corroboration, and likeliness.

I like journalists, and I respect what they do. Nonetheless, they and we operate differently. We plod a bit, poke here, think about it, consider what something means, look it over, check one more source. The journalist needs to hand in a story about the burning of the local Y—and by noon, thank you very much.

Oddly, and not clearly understood by others, there is a level of complexity posed by these seemingly innocent questions we are commonly asked. Some of the more thoughtful and interesting questions are often the easiest to answer, whereas some of the more specific questions require the greatest amount of work and worry.

I have been asked when Christmas became commercialized. This is an interesting topic, and I can give an answer that is general and yet helpful to a person seeking this information. In the 1890s, there was a definite increase in advertising in our local newspapers concerning Christmas. There are numerous illustrations, a great many large-type, eye-catching words such as "Christmas" and "presents" or "gifts," and even questions asking what the reader plans to give various members of the extended family, with suggestions for each. There are ads devoted to interesting and inexpensive gifts to be bought along State Street, and they are aimed at particular categories of people—such as fathers or children, second cousins and uncles. In addition, there is a good deal of rather bad verse celebrating the coming holiday.

Before the 1890s—in my community—the holiday was barely mentioned in the papers until the day or week before the twenty-fifth, and there was little notice afterward. And there was little said about gifts. Church services got much more attention than the offerings of Brown's Cheap Store or Rothschild Brothers' emporium. So this is a question I can answer from my general knowledge of the history of this place, and I can, with some certainty, send the interested party to old newspapers where examples can be found. On the other hand, a journalist rarely goes back to look at this sort of information him or herself.

It is often the simple-sounding questions that are more difficult, for they demand specificity of information. What is the history of the local Y? I could give a general outline, but without a file to consult or a history of the institution at hand, this question asks for details that must be verified. Others might know, but these are not the sorts of things that I carry about in my head or that I know with any certainty. Who were the people who brought the Y to the community? Where did the money come from? These require precision. What year was the building renovated, when was it relocated, and who was against the location of the new building? Of interest might be the sorts of programs offered, the number of children who were members, the year boarders ceased to be housed on the upper floors of the building, and when that small kitchen fire occurred. All these questions need precise answers, and most of us do not carry this sort of information around or even have it in a file by the telephone. If there has never been an article on the Y, or if the historian has never researched the question of the Y, then the answers to the legitimate questions above could take a considerable amount of time to gather.

We accommodate as best we can. Yet we cannot be expected to delve into intense research to answer a journalist's question. That is work that those in the media should do for themselves. Yet we know that they are up against deadlines and are only infrequently given much time to research a story. There is a dilemma here. A local historian told me recently that she was contacted just before a local election and asked about the racial composition of the city council if in this election certain candidates won. The reporter wanted to know if this would represent a unique situation. The historian's general knowledge would lead her to say yes, but she had no proof—at least not the sort of proof that historians require. To gather it would have entailed a long period of research in the records, and was this really her job? Put on the spot to give some sort of answer, she bravely said that she could not guess and that if an opinion were wanted, then the reporter should call a local politician who had been around for some time. In this case, the historian referred the journalist to someone who might be able to offer an answer. Had she done so herself, she feared that she might have been wrong and would, in any case, have had no proof with which to back up her "authoritative" answer.

FIRST THE EVIDENCE; THEN THE SERMON

Not long ago, a newspaper reprinted a student essay from a class on local history. The headline featured the phrase that the small city had a "well-earned early reputation as lawless and godless." The four-hundred-word article contained brief statements about a murder, trial, and execution. One sentence read that the "first murder trial occurred on Aug. 26, 1831, in a hotbed of sin, a town where churches struggled for survival." There are a number of problems with this. This 1831 episode was not the first murder committed in the region, nor the first execution in this particular part of the country; there had been other court-ordered executions earlier in places located within thirty miles and well within range of the part of the country described.

While the area had been frontier for approximately fifteen years, by the 1830s, the town being written about was the county seat, had four established churches with full congregations, and two new denominations in the process of forming. It was hardly a place where churches struggled for survival. Rather, it was a place that hoped to attract additional population. It sought more manufacturing companies and it looked forward to better links to markets. It had established political parties, though as in other places, they waxed and waned, and some people were subject to political fads. In the 1830s, it was probably no more or less sinful than other places nearby or distant.

While I take exception with the statements the student made, the student-writer is not really at fault. We learn by doing, and first and even early attempts—at art, music, and even history—are not always successful. This is where careful and dedicated teachers come in. In this case the teacher allowed a vague essay topic with a weak sense of chronology to pass without sufficient comment back to the student. The professor should have caught methodological inaccuracies in the student's essay. But there is more, for the teacher passed the essay to the local historical society, which passed it along to the local newspaper where it was published. There seemed to have been no vetting along the way!

The problem for me is that most people probably learn most of the local history they know from local newspapers. History essays have long been popular, especially in smaller papers that cater to a distinct geographic region. They remain popular today with a segment of the reading public. My unscientific assumption is that while some people ignore local history articles in a local newspaper, they are more likely to be read than books of local history, which are often bought but not read, bought for the illustrations, or bought as references rather than as reading material.

Local history that appears in the local paper is important. It is also generally regarded as true by readers by virtue of its appearance in the local paper, which lends its credibility to a local history article. (And goodness sakes, I don't want to go into what is truth here, please!)

When I read the essay cited above, I wrote a letter not intended for publication to the editor of the newspaper as a caution about unintended consequences. What follows is an example of what can happen.

Seventeen days after the appearance of the essay with the reference to the sinful community, there was a history article in another paper in the same community. That article's lead was "Violent history belies Peaceful Aura." Yikes! Here was another journalist writing about local history noting that beyond the façade of a picturesque community was the "haunting history of violence." The village, noted this second writer, was "populated by 'bootleggers, squatters, prostitutes, and other questionable characters," who lived in extreme poverty, "hunting, poaching, and relying on one another's good will to make ends meet." It ended with the comment that a particular man became the "first convicted murderer" in the region.

Much of the second article came straight from the first newspaper's story. One journalist picked up information, willy-nilly, from another without checking on the facts or asking any important questions, thereby blurring several different time periods together. I wrote another not-for-publication letter to the editors of this newspaper as well. And I should add, that rather than living in poverty, the local prostitute referred to lived rather well.

So here is the sermon.

Local history is interesting and it is fun. It can attract attention and help explain the past. Those of us engaged in local history are teachers of the community and also of students. We have a responsibility to ask clear questions, maintain historical standards, and to show how to do history well. We need to use our judgment to see that what is offered the public is done as carefully as possible.

There is, of course, a difference between what historians do and what journalists do, and how both camps seek information. The journalist may use the opinions of those they interview. This is not enough for historians, however, who must look at original materials, seek corroborating statements, look at the official records, seek secondary information for context, and look for comparisons and trends. This does not mean that historians are always right, for we are not. It does not mean, either, that journalists are not to be trusted, for they are.

In the case cited above, were I a reader unfamiliar with the history of a place, I would most certainly believe that in the 1830s, the community was a wild, woolly place full of violence and mayhem. That is what two newspapers have told readers, with one article bearing the imprimatur of a historical society—a trustworthy source. Of course readers believed what they read.

The moral of this is that newspapers are potent conveyors of local history. But another moral is that teaching requires responsibility, even if it is the hard task of showing an eager student what is wrong with an essay and how to improve it. It is definitely easy to give an A and to say, "Well done." It is much more difficult to actually know the material and to have historical standards that we pass along, not because we need to get every fact straight, but because students need to learn how to do good work so they set standards for themselves.

In this instance, the student's work did not receive responsible historical editing or criticism. The student's teachers are at fault, and so is the historical society that was so bent on publishing, whatever the content. Surely its archivist, historians, and curators should have read the essay critically before submitting it to the newspaper.

So what are we to do? How do we see that responsible essays are published, or do we let essays such as these simply slide by thinking that our own accounts will correct the record? Few people follow up a story to look for a correction in the next day's or next week's issue. Few people will really care.

But, actually, I care. I try very hard to get the story from the original sources. I make judgments about what the sources tell me. I try to get facts straight and to be true to the times about which I am writing. A week or so ago, a woman wrote to me that I had gotten wrong the names of a subject's brothers. Then she called and scolded me about publishing incorrect information. Then her sister wrote to say the same thing. I gave her the sources I had used—an obituary from a distant state, the local census, and Civil War regiment rosters. I publish locally with some frequency and I appreciate hearing from people who correct my stories if they need correcting, and who amplify things I write about. That is collaborative history gathering.

Two days after scolding me, the woman called again to say, "Oh, yeah, you were right and thanks, you saved us from making mistakes." That really pleased me. Not that I was right but that between us, we had gotten it right— or as right as we could. That was a teaching moment, what doing local history in the public arena is all about.

Sometimes I envy journalists their freedom not to worry about some of the things that tie me in knots. But I wouldn't be *them* for anything. I would rather work for the articles I write and feel confident that I did my best.

Local historians help when we can; we apologize when we cannot. But these situations are vexing, for journalists' questions often force us to use what we know in a way that sometimes violates how we historians believe we should function, and often these requests come with a time pressure that is unnatural to historians. However I respond to journalists' questions, I usually feel somewhat dissatisfied. Being asked by them, however, reaffirms my understanding of the historical method, and usually I am glad to do what I can to help.

Chapter Four

Clio and Her Sisters*

Many history presentations begin with a lecturer who shuffles papers and then begins to talk. Clio, the Muse of History, presents information and entertainment to an audience, and if one is lucky, she might be accompanied by her sister Calliope, the Muse of Eloquence. Sometimes, Calliope is missing from the presentation and Clio reads on.

There are other scenarios. Consider this: you enter a Beaux Arts building and go to an exhibit of items from an ancient Egyptian dynasty. There are on display some pots, clay tablets, and jewelry. They are varied items that are interesting or beautiful but objects that you might pass by with a quick glance, excepting that—on this day—there are also two saxophonists in the room who add their music, their presence, that make you slow down and consider the objects in front of you. Clio with Euterpe, the Muse of Music, enhance your experience.[1]

Or, consider this: you are in Mississippi, home of many hundreds of blues musicians from the early years of the twentieth century. Their lives were led, for the most part, in obscurity and poverty, set against the social and political limitations of the day. Yet, when you drive into Berclair, just a few miles south of Itta Bene, you can tune into the Mississippi Blues trail, created in 2009 to honor those musicians who have left almost nothing of a physical presence behind them in the way of houses or monuments, but whose music you can hear along with the story of their lives. B. B. King was born in Berclair. This collaboration between Clio and her sister Euterpe helps us recall and remember—and perhaps even understand in a deeper fashion—those who created this important American musical form.[2]

SOME DISCORD

Clio, the muse of history, however, does not always get on well with her sisters. Or they with her. Sometimes they want to dominate or do not want her to meddle with their lively constructions of the past. Sometimes, the mismatch has been created by a history organization that fails to provide historical context for its display of artworks, while at other times the fault lies with an arts organization or artist that fails to give historical context for its displays. Examples might be the George Catlin Indian Gallery displayed in Washington, D.C., or the Hudson River School paintings at the New-York Historical Society, both wonderful art exhibits but with woefully little commentary.

Public art sometimes results in disharmonies: the Chief Seattle statue, erected in 1912 in the heart of Seattle, might be a convenient icon but it also creates a problematic myth where solid history tells a somewhat different story. Public murals, today a popular form of conveying an episode from a community's past, can result in the artist using a historical moment but getting it somewhat wrong at the same time. In my hometown, there is a mural devoted to abolition heroes in which Frederick Douglass and Harriet Tubman are shown at opposite sides of the panel: Douglass is named in full and quoted, while Tubman is identified as "Comrade Tubman," a title that is anachronistic and misleading. This is especially sad because there are titles for Tubman that are descriptive and authentic; for example, she was known as the "Moses" of her people. Yet, artistic license prevents me from going out to erase the word "Comrade" and the artist refuses to make changes to his "concept." Here, history and the public lose out.

Film, a most popular and powerful art form, which might involve the muse Melpomene, the patron of tragedy, is also complicated. Melpomene is prone to enhance history and so too is her sister, Thalia, the Muse of comedy, as both are more often interested in attracting an audience than in getting the story straight. In a recent interview on PBS, film director Oliver Stone insisted on his right to present an "alternative myth," claiming that academic historians had hijacked the historical narrative, which, he believes, belongs to everyone. Ben Affleck, actor and director, in talking on *Fresh Air* about his 2012 film *Argo,* told Terry Gross that he believed that the "essential truth [is] part of story-telling," and he tried to "stay true to the essence" of his story. Yet, Maureen Dowd, writing in the *New York Times*, noted that in the film the last dramatic scene showing the Iranian Revolutionary Guard "jumping in a jeep, chasing the plane down the runway and shooting at it, was fabricated for excitement." Dowd also points out that the work of a "Sisterhood" of CIA employees were the ones who tracked down the whereabouts of Osama bin Laden, not just the single "Maya," who is portrayed as a solo operator in the movie *Zero Dark Thirty*.[3]

Nor is *Lincoln*, issued in 2012, without its flaws. The two House of Representatives members from Connecticut did not vote first on the Thirteenth Amendment, but they both voted "yea" whereas the film has them voting in the negative to enhance the tension of the moment. When alerted to this problem, Tony Kushner, the writer, thought it completely acceptable to "manipulate a small detail in the service of a greater historical truth. History doesn't always organize itself according to the rules of drama." I sympathize with the state of Connecticut about this: need that state be portrayed wrongly on such a momentous vote so that moviegoers can experience greater tension? Tragedy and Comedy might like it better this way, but Clio protests these missed opportunities to tell the story accurately and to find the drama in doing just that.[4]

On the other hand, sometimes members of the audience do not understand history and drama. A stage director told me of an audience member who quizzed an actor about the background of the role he was playing, asking him to explain the culture from which his character emerged. His response was one of disbelief that he was expected to know. He said that, "I studied the emotional needs of the role but I am not a historian." He explained, "I am brutal because it says so on page 1." His feeling was that no one had a right to expect him to know the historical basis of the play, as drama was not to be thought of as a history seminar.[5]

My friend Bill Hosley wrote that he thought "artists are almost disdainful of historical societies and perhaps history in general and that the heritage community is often clueless abut the power of art." He commented that on the other hand, historians are generally "weak on visuals and visual culture and Art Historians and the arts generally are weak on IDEAS and connectivity to the places they serve."[6] Would that it were otherwise: what a world it would be if they could be retrained to dance together, if Clio and Terpsichore, the Muse of Dance, might just get along.

CHANGES IN CULTURAL VALUE

An interesting thing has happened to Clio. In the nineteenth century, even more than philosophy, History was the stuff of our cultural currency—it was our common denominator. It was taught to instill patriotism and was a source of pride in that it gave proof that our home places were in some way special. Interest in history continued to engage Americans well into the twentieth century, during which time the number of history organizations went from 536 in 1930 to over seventeen thousand in 2009. Yet, today one is likely to hear that history is boring, that schoolteachers do not do a good job (something I totally dispute), that history is just "a bunch of dates"—another canard.

At the same time there has been an interesting rise in the cultural value of the arts (meaning a vast array of forms of creative expression), which began primarily as the interest of people of privilege but over time has been dramatically democratized. Art, in almost all of its forms, allows for and even encourages individual reaction. It was perfectly acceptable for individuals to like or dislike a particular piece, even without any education or knowledge about the artist, the times, or the genre. "I don't like that Warhol," one could say, or "I love that Winslow Homer."

Those crafty (in the best sense) museum people, however, provided a variety of ways to educate folks, using well-designed exhibits complete with labels, paper guides, and explanations, docents, classes, and even audio-tours that allow one to go at a personal pace through a gallery while learning about the objects displayed. Museum curators also courted the media, getting wonderful publicity for special shows called "blockbusters," promoting their artifacts as unique and a once-in-a-lifetime opportunity to see Monet's *Water Lilies*, for example, or objects from King Tut's tomb. They added to the actual experience take-aways in the form of stickers, program guides, and alluring gift shops. Art museums became destinations in themselves and developed a new cultural currency.

The interactivity of patron or viewer and display is important. Clio has attempted to provide opportunities in the form of interactive exhibits, walking tours, and trails. Last year in the *Denver Post*, however, Ray Mark Rinaldi commented that since the time of Duchamps, art has become more and more interactive, so much so that today one might go to an art exhibit and expect to touch or be encircled by fragments of art, bend to look into boxes at art, or to walk about and study the object under display. [7]

This recent trend for interactivity often centers on "Internet communities," focused on the "regular works on display so people can interact, or to add hands-on opportunities to major events," commented Rinaldi. He noted that in Denver the Art Museum often hosts a "studio" at the end of major shows so that visitors "can sit at a craft table, paint their own vase of flowers and hang it on the wall." He observes "their paintings are not very good, though maybe the act does make them feel closer to the artist, or just give them a chance to show off." The participant participates and therefore makes a connection with what he or she has seen. [8]

CURRENT HISTORY EXHIBITS

I believe all history exhibits incorporate art in some form, but few recent exhibits focus on the collaboration of Clio and her kith and kin. One way of understanding current trends is to look at the exhibits that have won recognition from The American Association for State and Local History (AASLH).

Awards certificates over the past three years have gone to exhibits that fall into several defined categories. Some feature Native peoples as living cultures ("Ever Changing, Ever the Same," at the Antelope Valley Indian Museum in California is one example); "Indians and Rusticators: Webanakis and Summer Visitors" is an exhibit that touches on the interaction of peoples in Maine.[9]

Another category of recent exhibits features ethnicity. There was a Basque exhibit in Boise, Idaho, that was shared with Ellis Island (2011), and in Maine an exhibit titled "Rivers of Imagination" featured the immigration to that state by Somalis and Bantus. In North Dakota, there was an exhibit that featured "Germans of Russian Heritage." Other current themes include exhibits that focus on gender, civil rights, and on spectacular events such as fires or mine disasters.

Architectural history is an area where art and history blend well, and a number of exhibits at historic houses won AASLH awards. "A Space for Faith: Colonial Meetinghouses" in New England and "Remarkable Homes" in Wisconsin are but two.

Few of these exhibits, however, are purposeful collaborations between history and art excepting the AASLH winner, "Becoming Modern," about the twentieth-century artist Wharton Esherick, created in a partnership between the Wharton Esherick Museum in Paoli, Pennsylvania, the library and architectural archives at the University of Pennsylvania, and the Hedgehog Theater Company.

Joining history and the arts can have wonderful results but it also takes effort, and while larger historical organizations might have staff to take on the task, many small historical societies have scant staff or are run by volunteers. A large or small organization, however, might put together a photo squad of folks who like to take pictures or who belong to a local Photographers Guild. Have these folks document the present, especially changes occurring in our hometowns. They might focus on destructions and constructions, on people and places, events and happenings, and these images could be displayed with comments by the photographer about what he saw, what she thought about when taking the picture, or even, what the picture means to the community. It is important to generate this sort of interaction.

A small organization might exhibit local paintings of place and have painters and visitors tell stories about the scenes. Main Street might be seen as a changing local canvas, from the store names, to the changes in the contents and purpose of shops, to the advance of technology and advertising.

I am always impressed when people, such as the folks in Florida or those in Texas, use the radio to present historical moments. In Florida the PBS station airs history segments; in Texas, famous women from the state are highlighted in short spots on the radio.[10]

Eating is an art. I am a fan of "Eating Around," a way of taking history into local restaurants, especially those that feature a defined cuisine, where that culture is the focus, including dance and music in addition to the food, but also using that opportunity to talk about changes in the local demography. We involve not only food and the history of food, but also Terpsichore and Euterpe.

What about holding a poetry slam in a graveyard? Just think about *Spoon River Anthology* and even *Our Town*. The poets might be encouraged to find out something about the person whose grave they are assigned to; the audience gets to hear a poem and appreciate the art and decoration in a graveyard and to see it as public space.

Clothing presents opportunities: 1960s outfits, the clothing of sport, the collections we have without even thinking about them: of shoes, of dresses. "Out of the Closet" would provide an opportunity for a small organization to invite teens to create an exhibit of what they think represents their own times, and to comment on the objects they select. This would give them an opportunity to show other generations what they value, and also an insight into what creating an exhibit is all about. It might help the rest of us to understand their clothing choices!

There are important history themes, also, especially those from the twentieth century that we share and should be tapped by all of us. One of my favorites concerns the appearance of the automobile and how it changed lives. "Driving About" would involve people in how the automobile created a road etiquette; necessitated road and street signs, changing our visual landscape; was also the object of scorn, admiration, and even accidents—and these were written about in a variety of ways: as a caution about this newfangled machine, as a sign of change, as a new way of thinking about time and space. Our language changed because of the automobile, and so did courting. Do see Beth Bailey's lovely book *From the Front Porch to the Back Seat* (1989).[11]

There is also an important theme concerning the democratization of opportunity in politics, education, and civil wrongs and rights. Democratization allows us to talk about change in time and place and can be created from newspaper articles, letters from students away at school, by means of protest posters, and especially of voting patterns amid the growing diversity of our population.

Another important theme has to do with the abandonment of rural spaces. Our farms have changed over time. They smell different than they did in the previous century; they are operated differently, and owned often these days by outsiders. Farm family structure has also changed, with more members of the family earning a living off the farm. These are subjects that local historical societies can take on—sometimes by presenting an exhibit, but more often, I hope, by talking with friends and neighbors about changes in the community and how to document them, what they mean to those of us still there, what these rural changes mean to small commercial centers.

And of course, there are the important issues raised by changes in family life. We could look at real estate advertisements to see what modern families value in a house, at technology to see how it has altered the family, and at the family itself, its home, its structure, its function, as it undergoes changes sometimes sought and sometimes thrust unwarranted upon it.

Each of these large themes should be considered merely headings under which topics of concern to a community could be tackled. They offer a framework for many and varied modes of presentation, of artifact collection; they beg for oral history, material culture studies, and most especially for the participation of all people in the community, not just curators or museum directors, but board members, druggists, and housewives.

THE SERMON

I think it is most important to remember why we research and collect and work to present the past—why we engage with Clio and her sisters even while in collaboration there are pitfalls. There are actually wonderful reasons to work together.

We do not do these things just to get people in the doors of our museums, or to lure tourists to see our house museums, or to prove our economic value to our communities. These benefits should happen but they are not the goal. I believe we do these things, and other activities such as writing articles, publishing pamphlets, exhibiting local products, providing lecture space, inviting the public in, to add the voice of experience to local situations. We do these things because we history-organization folks have the means of providing a way to understand and appreciate and contribute to—and yes, to enjoy and understand—place. We are the folks who can help individuals see themselves in time and over time—to understand that they are often tossed by historical currents and often buck those tides to go their own ways. We can help people understand where they are in time and place, and to know that others too once lived here and used the land, made opportunities for themselves, created lives: lived in our houses and planted in our gardens, as we do today, adding our own presence for those who come after.

Twenty-five years ago, wanting to celebrate an anniversary, we gave residents of my city and county a challenge. We invited them to participate in the "One Day" project and on May 17, 1988, everyone in the community was invited to write about his or her day, to observe life around them, to describe what our place meant to them. This was a project inspired by Maxim Gorky, who in 1935 asked fifty writers to consider our common humanity. The times were difficult; the world was sliding toward another war. Gorky hoped that what was shared about our lives, in Poland and Portugal, in Timor and Timbuktu, would stem the tide of war. It didn't work, of course, and World War II happened.

But from the Russian experiment, the Chinese had the idea of asking all literate people in that country to write about one day, describing the world around them, in effect, to speak not only for themselves but in 1936 for all those in China who were not literate and could not write of their own lives. The Chinese received four thousand entries and published a book containing some three hundred essays.

The Ithaca One Day exercise played off the Chinese example. The most startling entry was from a woman whose mother had been a Shanghai student in 1936 and who had submitted her essay about the street life she passed on her way to school. Our book opened with the mother's 1936 essay and her daughter's from 1988. The reason I mention this is because when we published 180 essays in a book called *One Day in Ithaca* we had a party for those whose articles were included. At that occasion, almost every one of the authors said to me, "Thank you." Puzzled, I said that I thanked them for participating but asked them why they were thanking me. Their answer was universal: we participated and wrote our essays because no one had ever asked us before; we had never felt a part of the history of this place. Now, twenty-five years later, we repeated this exercise but this time with computer and phone and easy access to the wonders of photography.[12]

It is for that sense of wonder and appreciation that every life matters that we do what we do. It is why we need to always remember to ask those around us what they think, what they are interested in, what they would like to see exhibited, and why. We need to always remember to ask the public for its opinion, its participation.

The Muses are part of a complicated family. They sing the memory of what is, what was, and what will be. To the Greeks, memory was truth. The ancient poets invoked the Muses so that their songs would be considered veracious and that into them they might breathe the imperishable memory and knowledge that the Muses alone can bestow: false songs would cause them to become mute. What we know and tell about the places we live, the experiences of people and place, the trials and joys are enhanced when Clio and her sisters are inspired to create and fashion truthful songs.

Clio and her sisters have much to offer us. They expand the ways that history can be communicated, they encourage us to invite others to join us in the challenge of educating, enriching, enticing, entertaining and engaging people with the past, and with their own times. Clio and her sisters acting respectfully and cooperatively can give the people of our hometowns the opportunity to know themselves better, to understand place, and to contribute to the future.

* This chapter reprinted with the permission of the Washington State Historical Society and the thoughtfulness of Shanna Stevenson, who suggested that I speak about this topic. I am not sure the talk turned out quite the way Shanna expected, but it was a rewarding experience for me to put this together. I also relied on a number of friends for advice, especially Mary Alexander, who has always responded to my questions with wisdom and generosity.

NOTES

1. Mary Alexander, director of the Museum Advancement Program at the Maryland Historical Trust, described this experience to me. I appreciate conversations with Mary about this topic, and indeed, over the years, about many topics that involve history and how we convey it to the public.

2. You can learn about the Mississippi Blues trail at http://blues.goodbarry.com/locations/b-b-king-birthplace-map.

3. On January 5, 2013 Chris Hayes of MSNBC interviewed Oliver Stone on his program *Up*. See Maureen Dowd, "The Oscar for Best Fabrication," *New York Times*, February 17, 2013, page 11 in the "Week in Review." And see Scott Magelssen and Rhona Justice-Mallory, eds., *Enacting History* (Tuscaloosa: University of Alabama Press, 2011) in which they discuss a variety of theatrical ways of using (and misusing) history, from the Ping Chong "Undesirable Elements/Secret Histories," the stories of marginalized peoples, to battle reenactments, historical performances such as the Sioux City, Iowa, pageant about Lewis and Clark, medieval festivals, and the immersion experience at Conner Prairie.

4. Dowd, "The Oscar for Best Fabrication," 11.

5. Conversation with Rachel Lampert, artistic director of The Kitchen Theater, Ithaca, New York, January 23, 2013.

6. Email from William Hosley, December 29, 2012. Hosley is the president of Terra Firma Northeast based in Connecticut.

7. Ray Mark Rinaldi, "Art and the Active Audience: Participatory Art Changes Audience Role from Viewer to Doer," *Denver Post*, December 31, 2012, denverpost.com. Recent interactive exhibits include "Ann Hamilton's 'the event of a thread,'" in New York City; in Colorado Springs there was Eiko and Koma's "Residue of Nakedness;" and in Louisville, there was "21C," a concept that combined a museum and a luxury hotel. Even religious congregations see value in partnering with art; see Amy O'Leary, "Building Congregations around Art Galleries and Cafes as Religiosity Wanes," *New York Times*, December 30, 2012.

8. Rinaldi, "Art and the Active Audience."

9. See AASLH.org for lists of exhibit and program winners and for instructions and applications that your programs be considered.

10. See AASLH.org for its list of outstanding exhibits. In 2012, Texas was given an award for its Texas Women's History Moments; for the use of radio in Florida, see Ben Brotemarkle, "Florida, local history in," in *Encyclopedia of Local History*, Carol Kammen and Amy H. Wilson, eds. (Lanham, MD: AltaMira Press, 2012), 192–94.

11. Beth Bailey, *From the Front Porch to the Back Seat: Courtship in Twentieth-Century America* (Baltimore: Johns Hopkins University Press, 1989).

12. See *One Day in Ithaca: May 17, 1988*, Carol Kammen, ed. (Interlaken, NY: Ithaca Centennial Committee, 1989).

Chapter Five

How to Write a Congregational History*

History needs to begin with a question. Most local histories of communities touch on the establishment of religious congregations and provide information relating to the formation of a church, in particular its denominational definition. Congregational histories, for their part, often go into details about ministers' lives; ever-present financial needs; its buildings and their demise (especially by fire), their expansion, or replacement; and whether the congregation created or supported any guilds, societies, or missions. They are a virtual who's who, or who was who, of the congregation.

Local community histories and histories of a single congregation often overlook each other's significance. Both manage, in fact, to miss the other almost entirely. A local history will often cite the appearance of a new religious denomination but will have little more to say about it than that. A congregational history generally discusses its ministers, its financial struggles, its identity: did it change denominations, or suffer a schism? These bones of a congregational history are just that: bones. They often lack a substantial, satisfying context—what we might call the *meat* of a history. If we can bring joint and flesh together, we can reach the crux of what is interesting and important in congregational histories and place the church in its evolving local setting. What is written is determined by the questions that are asked.

History can begin with a simple question, like "When was this congregation formed?" The more complex the question, however, the more interesting the results. Consider the richer narrative that would result from asking "Why was this congregation formed in this place when it was? And, by whom?" Or, to push the question a bit further, "What does the formation of this congregation say about the founders and what they expected a church would mean to their lives and to the community?" Keep in mind that early religious organizations, especially in frontier locations, were some of the first social organizations in an area to provide a sense of stability and order. After exploring these meatier questions about the congregation's beginnings, the next step might be to discover what difference this church made to the community around it and how community developments were reflected within the congregation.

A LOCAL EXAMPLE

This is a bone of history: in 1804, two frontier ministers charged to bring religion to "needy places" organized a Presbyterian congregation of thirteen persons at the head of Cayuga Lake in a community that came to be called Ithaca. To get to the flesh takes more effort. We could begin by digging deeper for contextual information, which would borrow from—and eventually add to—the local history of the place. The initial congregation was small but in 1805 a Dutch Reformed minister connected to the major landowner arrived in the hamlet and was installed as its first pastor. He served the lakeside congregation and also another eleven miles to the north, visiting each on alternative Sundays. This arrangement lasted until 1812, during which time there was little increase in the congregation and Ithaca was described by a church historian as an "inconsiderable place, [and] wickedness greatly prevailed," whereas the landowner had a more optimistic and enterprising view of the place.[1] By 1815 the "Dutch Dominee" had moved away, leaving the Ithaca congregation on its own in an area still considered frontier. This is some of the meat of the story of the congregation and also of the small community.

This is a good time to consider the forces at work in that time and place. We could remember the importance of doctrinal differences, and also remember the Plan of Union of 1801, enacted to lessen competition between Presbyterians and Congregationalists. We could delve into the social and economic stresses of a frontier community struggling to grow out of disorder, that it might become a settled place attractive to manufacturers, lawyers, businessmen and their families.

What would that transition take? Some sought a stable community, but even with improvements, "other vices prevailed,"[2] for at the same time some in the community resisted religious or social restraints as they were interested in making money by selling liquor to the teamsters (drivers of teams of draft animals) and others who were then streaming through the area. All, of course, expected to do well on this new land, to achieve material satisfaction, but some equated the frontier as a place without the social (and religious) constraints associated with more settled parts of the country. Still others professed a different form of religious belief, and some none at all.

Back to our Ithaca example: in 1816, the church congregation in Ithaca contained fewer than thirty people. The new minister, William Wisner, young and eager, rode in like the hero of an epic story, looking for evil to fight, and he finds it among those attending the Presbyterian meetings. He expels two leading gamblers, the Swedenborgians, and the imbibers. This earns him some enemies; some of those banished from the flock white-washed the new minister's horse and burned down the schoolhouse in which the congregation met. But he persevered; he pulled together the acceptable few, converted two of the horse-racers, and by 1825 had a congregation of 263, and states in a memoir that the "morals of the place were greatly improved."[3]

This is a success story well worth telling, but it is not the whole story. A more complete history would explore how the success of the congregation was tied to the transformation of the community as it increased in population and stability. So, at this point, the community historian needs to intercede. The Reverend William Wisner did not change the character of the population at the head of Cayuga Lake by himself. The small community, formless and without government when Wisner arrived, had been designated by the state in 1817 as the seat of a new county—and isn't that interesting? It turns out the state surveyor general, Simeon DeWitt, nephew of New York Governor George Clinton, owned most of the land along the lakeshore, and he was the one in Albany drawing the new county lines. He also stood to profit by the sale of land in the new county seat, and he promoted Ithaca to those looking for new lives in New York's attractive Finger Lakes region.

Most people in the lakeside community had an interest in this venture; they saw an opportunity to make something of their rowdy settlement, sometimes called Sin City or Sodom. These people believed that few settlers, even fewer manufacturers or investors, and certainly not the Bank of Newburg, would be interested in a branch in Sin City. They understood that it was in everyone's interest that the adolescent ways of the community be set aside and a more proper village emerge in its place. Many helped to achieve this transformation, including a group called the Moral Society that put down lawlessness. We begin to understand that the Presbyterian congregation and local conditions cannot be meaningfully discussed one without the other, though they generally are. By fleshing out these intersections, we have just given the bones of the church's creation story some very tasty meat.

A QUESTIONABLE HERO

At this point, we need to look Reverend William Wisner straight in the eye. Originally the hero of this story, he doesn't necessarily remain that way. According to the church records and memoirs by those who knew him, Wisner's manner was rigid and unbending, sometimes a difficult fit with a community in the midst of major change. While he was revered by some, others complained that his "Calvinistic meat was too strong" and they "could endure it no longer."[4] We must also wonder why in 1822 thirty or so members of the congregation left to become Anglicans and were glad to get out from under Reverend Wisner's authority. In 1830, more than thirty-one members left to create a Dutch Reformed Church, motivated by more than wanting to preserve their own linguistic heritage. In their church minutes they called Wisner "pope," not a compliment in a community that harbored an unseemly anti-Catholicism as waves of Irish immigrants began arriving. That this Presbyterian congregation became the mother of other churches was not necessarily a reflection of Presbyterian success but rather of discontent among parts of the congregation.

In the 1904 Presbyterian history,[5] Wisner is described as an old-fashioned divine, spouting hell and brimstone, but not as someone who drove people away. Several decades later, when he refused to allow a discussion of abolition within the church, he expelled or drove off yet another group who became Congregationalists and formed what has locally been called the "Abolition Church."

Reverend Wisner is a complicated character. When we read his published sermons we find strong opinions on a number of issues: he criticized fairs and festivals as being Roman Catholic in origin; he opposed the idea of post offices being open on Sunday; he opposed abolition activity, considering the subject of slavery a secular matter outside the reach of the church. Yet none of the researchers who collectively wrote the Presbyterian history published in 1904 referenced these sermons. The meat, in these cases, is a bit tainted. It doesn't reflect well on Wisner or his congregational supporters, the elders and deacons and their prominent families. In providing a richer history, we sometimes find our historical subjects are more complicated than we'd like. This is interesting and a bit troublesome.

Wisner's motivation was probably to succeed and escape the small village and thereby advance in the Presbyterian hierarchy; he got as far as Rochester but returned to Ithaca for another stint before going off to Cedar Rapids, where he eventually died. His body was returned to Ithaca, however, and he is buried in the City Cemetery, among his many parishioners.

So what have we learned? The Presbyterian Church provided community leadership and stability, but it also responded somewhat narrowly to diversity of opinion from within the congregation, causing some congregants to leave, and to the issue of slavery that roiled a number of church members and some of those in the community. We've learned that this congregation's history is connected to the growth of a number of other local Protestant churches. We also have to remember that many people, especially from the "best families," may have remained Presbyterian in part because of the social status associated with this congregation, others because of their feeling of belonging within the denomination. A rich, meaty history of a "successful" congregation may be a complicated one.

Moving to the twentieth century, we can again use the lens of history to examine the congregation. How did Presbyterians in the Ithaca church react to the Civil Rights movement? Did they support draft resisters who protested at the nearby post office? What was their response to the rallies against the war in Vietnam that took place in the adjacent park, which is actually church property? How did they feel about women preachers? When New York passed its first law allowing abortions, what was the Presbyterian stand? The Presbyterian history published in 2009 to commemorate the church's second hundred years, again a group effort, raises none of these issues.[6]

In examining church affairs, we find ties to the larger world. For example, when the sale of a piece of property in 1998 brought the church a windfall, the minister invited each member to help divvy it up by proposing a ministry to support. As a result, some money went to local efforts but a large proportion went to foreign missions. This is a lovely topic to explore! There are also questions we can ask about how the congregation faced doctrinal and ministerial changes; how the congregation dealt with financial issues; how they worked together to solve problems or experienced schisms. In recent history, there may be members of the congregation who remember and can report on these topics.

In whatever time period we research, using a variety of lenses, we're trying to discover the church's role in its home community.

LITTLE IS STRAIGHTFORWARD

A history of a church, denomination, or religious group is a complicated affair. We are looking for what happened and what didn't happen, and our sources must come from within the church and from without. Our questions should highlight the role of the church as solace to the individual soul, to the congregational whole, and as a responder to the social issues of the day. This makes the history of the church a living document full of the Sturm und Drang of life, not just a testament to the health of the congregation.

SO HOW *DO* YOU WRITE A CONGREGATIONAL HISTORY?

Start by asking questions that really interest you. How did your congregation react to the struggle between the Fundamentalists and Modernists?[7] How did the congregation find money to rebuild when the church burned down the day after the insurance ran out? What are the continuities in the congregation's history and what are the bumps along the road that disjoint the present from the past?

Bones

Discover what is already known (names of pastors, church locations, special projects like missionary efforts). There's no need to redo the work already done, and you will most likely find plenty of bones lying about. Consider yourself a dog on a hunt. Once you have your bones, you can get to your more interesting questions.

Moving Ahead

Decide who will be involved and how. One person or a group may write a congregational history, either as volunteers or an individual or even a company hired by the congregation. A group of congregants, however, might want to be involved in the project, each bringing enthusiasm, knowledge, and concern about the congregation. These people might consider themselves the History Gang. They may be led by coleaders or even a local academic, historian, or experienced writer. Even if they convene as a leaderless group, they may be better served by some formal leadership scheme agreeable to all. A leader would set schedules, parcel out work assignments, and ensure that discussions are gently conducted. Each participant should understand that while some history chores might be completed quickly, a book project will most realistically take between two to three years, if a book is the goal.

Not everyone in the History Gang will want to be involved with writing, but everyone should be interested in researching, and discussing what their discoveries mean and how they all fit together. All should be invited to try drafts if they care to, though some will be more avid and capable than others. These drafts should be read by all and discussed. Some will be gently discarded, others blended into a final version. It is important to remember that even a large project consists of a great many small parts to which a variety of people can bring their talents. This is where leadership will be especially important. In my experience most people know what they can accomplish and what might be daunting.

Keeping Accounts

Before the History Gang begins to research, there are some useful tasks to take on, and some important discussions to have. One of these concerns is documenting what is found. There is general knowledge that does not need to be footnoted. We do not have to assure or even reassure readers that a county was formed at a specific date, or that an external event, such as the Great War or the Great Depression, happened. We do need to footnote new information or new interpretations, assertions where we differ from others who have written on the subject, or where we have found the proof for our own statements. There are people who make a fuss about footnotes—they don't like them and think readers don't like them. I consider footnotes useful, just as the rungs on a ladder are necessary for getting to the top. I am not strident, however, about form as long as all research notes carry basic information: most especially, where the information is from and where it can be found by others.

The purpose of footnotes is to leave a trail that others may follow. They might expand on your information in their own work, or they might disagree with your conclusions, but that is their business. Not every project requires footnotes; you won't need them for a card in a Sunday program or a radio spot, but you would want credits at the end of a video presentation. Citations allow others to see what process you used and, most important, they serve better than your own memory if you have to explain how you know what you're saying. Believe me, it is far easier to keep track of where you have looked as you go along than to have to go back at some point to figure out where your information came from.

The Importance of Reading

Begin by reading a local history, even if it is a bad or dull one. You are bound to learn something, if only what not to do. It will give you a frame within which to think and work. You might chart some important things about the locality: population trends, disasters, major issues. Discuss these within the group. I have a congregational history on my desk, covering the years 1904 to 2004, with a chart that lists selected major events—but it has some major problems. Church events listed on the chart begin in 1963, and while there are some national items there are no local events. What about our local flood of 1935 or the regional flood of 1972 that devastated a nearby community? These are significant local events. Were the Presbyterians involved with relief efforts for those who suffered?

Reading a history of the Presbyterian Church will also provide more information for your chart, and a guide to national issues, religious controversies, and triumphs—and will help you figure out the differences (and subsequent mergers) among the various Presbyterian branches. The online Presbyterian Historical Society timeline (www.history.pcusa.org) is a very helpful beginning. One entry on the timeline reads:

> 1892 Charles Briggs, brilliant and argumentative professor at Union Seminary, NY, is embroiled in one of the most publicized heresy trials in the church's history due to his "higher-critical" views of Scripture. Reacting to the controversy, the General Assembly adopts language defending the "inerrancy" of Scripture.

From this we learn that Briggs triggered a controversy and the General Assembly responded. To learn more you need to consult a general history of the church.[8] Read the previous history of the congregation—there usually is one. Now that you have a skeleton chart of local events, are there parallels between community and church, or national church history and the local congregation? Did your local congregation have an opinion on the 1892 controversy? It might have had, but then the whole episode might have gone without notice in the records.

Read the histories of other community congregations. To be truthful, congregational historians almost never do this but it is really important. Sometimes what others report will highlight a local event, offering you a chance to compare your congregation's involvement. The other reason to read—or skim—through other church histories is to see your congregation reflected in the eyes of others. This is how I learned about how others viewed Reverend Wisner. The Ithaca Dutch Reformed secretary in the church minutes called Wisner a "pope." The history of St. John's Parish (Episcopalian) notes that the resolution to establish a church in Ithaca came about in 1821, after two men with Anglican backgrounds listened to Reverend William Wisner, who they called a "pugnacious divine of the old hell-fire school," make "a rabid attack" upon the Episcopal Church.[9] These words fired up the two men, who went on to found their own Anglican religious establishment in Ithaca. In addition, if we read further in the two short pamphlets detailing the history of the Unitarian Church in Ithaca, we find that Wisner preached against the Unitarians and refused to meet the new pastor. When Wisner fell ill, however, Reverend Stebbins of the Unitarian congregation went to visit him. Surprised, Reverend Wisner said "Well, you may not be a Christian; but your [sic] the first minister in town to come and see me."[10] See what we have learned? I'll bet not one Presbyterian in my city knows any of this! That is the value of reading other denominational histories.

You might also observe what other church histories do well and what they do not do at all. Where are their emphases? These other histories could be parceled out among the History Gang members and each could report on one. Most tend to be short, if that is an encouragement.

If there are few or no printed histories of other congregations, consult the local historical archive, as it is sure to have a file on religious organizations within the locality. Discuss what others consider important, what others do well, and think about what interested you and what parts you skipped over. All this reading might feel as if you are *not* writing a congregational history, but you will write a better one if you do this.

Discuss What You Learn

Do not read in a vacuum. You need to talk with each other about what you find, discuss which items are good and those that are less than thrilling, figure out which local or national events caused congregations to act together, and note when congregations turned a blind eye to a startling need you learned of in your reading about the community. Do any of these histories talk about poverty? Can you track the interesting and important change, from the end of the nineteenth century and into the twentieth, in the concept of philanthropy—progressing from helping one's family, neighbors, and members of a congregation to a more general concern for the community at large? This was sometimes accompanied by the creation of orphan asylums and homes for elderly women and other institutions that addressed social need and out of it grew the idea of public responsibility: benevolence from the healthy, wealthy, and wise (as well as Presbyterian) to the indigent, improvident, invalid—and inebriated. This shift sometimes happened with congregational support and sometimes outside the context of the religious community. In my community, joint efforts at addressing public need came in the 1870s by women from all the local religious congregations who banded together to tackle social ills, which they did quite spectacularly. The question here is: When did the congregation begin to regard people outside of it as their responsibility? How did we develop a community or public conscience? This is a stunningly important question. How does your church fit into it?

Additional Information

With organized notes and some local history under your belt, there is the question of where to look for more information. The church will have created, over time, a goodly amount of material about its activities: minutes, scrapbooks, special reports, white papers, disorganized (or even organized) files. The church office or library is the place to start.

The local historical society will have some items, perhaps even a lot. Presbyterian churches also submit reports, so don't forget to see what is available at the Presbyterian Historical Society.[11] The historical society maintains a comprehensive website, but I would talk with a reference librarian to see how to begin to use the printed and manuscript materials described in CALVIN, the electronic catalog. Asking librarians and archivists for advice is always rewarding, as is asking local experts. People like being able to help, and it allows them to show off what they know. Your question should be, however, "how can I find out" rather than "tell me everything you know." You are seeking aid in becoming a congregational historian; you are not a leech.

Other materials to consult include the local newspaper, the federal census, the personal papers of people associated with the congregation, and old photographs. Oral history has become fashionable and it is a fine way of connecting with more recent events. [12]

Advice and Advisors

Consult local experts: community-college faculty members, historical society archivists, and local writers or teachers. One of these might lead your history effort; others might be available to consult from time to time. Some might read over your early writing efforts. It is good to have a batch of folks in your corner—they need not all be Presbyterian.

History Can Be Delivered in Many Forms

Once you have some context it is time to figure out how you want to proceed. Consider alternate ways of telling the congregation's history. We are in the twenty-first century—and you do not have to choose only one. While having a book in your hand to show for your work is a source of momentary pride (and often some chagrin, and then regret, and then the humiliation of having to sell the darn thing), but it might not be the most effective means of conveying a congregation's history. You might consider an online chronology that can become a cumulative site, added to by others as time goes by, or a series of pamphlets on particular topics (church architecture, women's work over time, or topically, the church during the era of Civil Rights, missionary activities, the church today). I am a particular fan of pamphlets as they allow you to produce history in segments, either chronologically or by subject, with little expense. Also think about creating a video presentation, or a digital history on a disc with a good number of images. More creatively, you could develop a set of cards with important church characters on them, or a game for youngsters. Writing and staging a drama is a wonderful way of bringing history alive. There could be some local issues that deserve an article in a state history journal, a local newspaper, or in the *Journal of Presbyterian History*. Radio spots, displays for the church lobby, or card-sized historical anecdotes for the Sunday bulletin are a few more formats.

You might also want to write a book. There is no right way, but there will be ways that suit your situation and those working on recovering the history and communicating it. Remember that the materials needed for a book are different than those required for different formats. Whatever you decide, remember to organize and preserve your research materials in a dependable, local archive.

Documenting Your Work

Create your own archive as you work and then see that it is preserved in a safe place, preferably a local or regional library. If you have a group working on a congregational history, one individual might assume the role of archivist, checking that sources are marked on all materials, keeping information in a logical progression, and noting where information is missing.

What You Will Gain

There are benefits beyond creation of the actual historical work about your congregation. Everyone who works on the project will develop increased awareness about how history is created, how events unfold, and may read books and newspapers with an increased appreciation. All will learn about your church, about the church in time and space, and about the community. Mostly, you will learn about yourselves—an important lesson. Writing a congregational history is not an act of faith, as some books imply. Your faith is your business; writing a church history is an act of recovery and honesty. It's important to those in the pews beside you and to people all over town, but it is also a gift to the future. Writing a church history is a way of honoring the past, informing the present, and showing the future that people in time and place matter—that individual actions sometimes change the path of history, and that joining together has consequences that matter to us all.

There Be Dragons—One in Particular

There is also danger. Some people will not like your choices; that is their prerogative. Some on the team will consider the project complete when their part is finished, and will go off to do other things. But beware, for scouring the past, looking into corners, and delving into motivations is addictive. Consider that this is habit forming, life changing, and that topics for research are endless.

One way to feed your habit is to consider how the present will be remembered. The experience of delving into the past and encountering sources that don't pan out, leads that go nowhere, and looking for documents that don't exist will make you think about how to record what is going on *now*. History never stops: the past is yesterday. We live in the midst of history. What we create today is what people in the future will know about us. We can leave behind only bones of today, or we can collect for the future and document the dilemmas of today, the issues we face, the opinions voiced in committees, the life stories and pictures of those among us now, and the attempts we all make to cope with the world we are in. Such could be the result of writing a congregational history—and that's not at all a bad meal!

*This chapter was originally commissioned by the Presbyterian Historical Society.

NOTES

1. James A. Hotchkin, *A History of the Purchase and Settlement of Western New York and of the Rise, Progress, and Present State of the Presbyterian Church in that Section* (New York, 1848), 409. See Simeon DeWitt letters of 1810 in William Heidt, Jr. and Carol Kammen, eds., *Simeon DeWitt, Founder of Ithaca* (Ithaca: DeWitt Historical Society, 1968).

2. Hotchkin, *A History of the Purchase and Settlement of Western New York*, 409.

3. See S. J. Parker, *A Picture of Ithaca, N.Y. as I saw it in Childhood*, an unpublished manuscript in the Cornell University Library, Rare and Manuscript Collection, and partially reprinted in Carol Kammen, ed., *What They Wrote: 19th Century Documents from Tompkins County, New York* (Ithaca, NY: Department of Manuscripts and University Archives, Cornell University Libraries, 1978), 12–13.

4. *History of the First Presbyterian Church of Ithaca, New York, During One Hundred Years* (Ithaca, 1904), 21.

5. *History of the First Presbyterian Church of Ithaca, New York, During One Hundred Years* (Ithaca, 1904), 21.

6. *100 Years of Reflections: 1904–2004*, Pat Leach, editor, (Ithaca, NY: First Presbyterian Church, 2009).

7. This is a topic thoughtfully considered in "The Pastoral Vision of Martin Hardin," an essay by John H. Weiss that concludes *100 Years of Reflections*, pages 77–80.

8. The most recent books are Thomas Matthew Gilliland, *Truth and Love: The United Presbyterian Church of North America: A Fifty Year Retrospective* (2008); Randall H. Balmer and John Fitzmier, *The Presbyterians* (1994); or James H. Smythe, *A Brief History of the Presbyterian Church* (1996). Then, of course, look in your church minutes to see what reaction your congregation might have had to all this (no reaction is also interesting information).

9. Ralph C. H. Catterall, *Ninety Years of St. John's Parish: Ithaca, NY* (1912: from an address given in celebration of the ninetieth anniversary of the founding of the Parish, with supplemental notes), unpaged pamphlet.

10. Okay, let's deal with sic right now: we insert sic, a word from Latin meaning "thus," into the text to indicate that the expression or spelling exactly reproduces the original. That means it is not our mistake, but it is their rendering. In this case the writer meant to say "you are," or "you're," not the possessive "your." They all sound very much the same in our confusing English, but we know the difference. Use sic. It will make you feel comfortable about what you report.

11. 425 Lombard Street, Philadelphia, Pennsylvania 19147, by phone at (215) 627-1852 and on the Internet at http://www.history.pcusa.org/.

12. Two extremely useful anthologies of articles and essays on oral history are Willa Baum and David Dunaway, *Oral History: An Interdisciplinary Anthology*, 2nd ed. (Walnut Creek, CA: AltaMira Press, 1996) and Robert Perks and Alistair Thomson, *The Oral History Reader*, 2nd ed. (New York: Routledge, 2006). There is also a useful essay on oral history in the second edition of *The Encyclopedia of Local History* (2012), which contains other interesting essays about doing local history.

Chapter Six

Researching Local History

This single circumstance of want of materials, would, in the absence of all other reasons, justify us in receiving with extreme distrust, the narratives of the earliest historians. Before the art of printing was invented few documents existed, and tradition furnishes almost the only materials for history. How much falsehood gathered in its progress, and how much truth, modifying and almost changing the aspects of the truths it transmitted; was lost on the way, could only be the subject of conjecture.
—Salma Hale, "An Address, Delivered before the New-Hampshire Historical Society, at the Annual Meeting, 11th June 1828"[1]

Everything that men and women have written, touched, or made is a clue to the past, as are thoughts, memories and intangible constructions, such as organizations, communities, designs, plans. Such a wide range of material demands of the local historian a variety of talents so that this evidence will yield up its secrets. We need to do more than simply accept the flotsam of the past: we must question it, consider it, evaluate possible reasons for its creation, and wonder why it has survived. Although this is an obvious way to approach a historical artifact, it is not one regularly used by all historians—a lack that has led to problems for even the most careful researcher. Many times, that which the past has given us controls our view of a particular era or episode. Let me try to illustrate this.

Many communities (and most secretaries of state's offices) have business incorporation papers for a mill, a business, or a small manufactory. The local historian, by dint of hard work, may discover a sales ledger, advertisements in a newspaper about the product, and even some of the products that have survived as collectors' items: clocks, bottles, tinware, pottery jugs, and the like. Put together, this varied information leads to the study of a local business—a worthwhile undertaking and a relatively common local history pro-

ject. The incorporation papers for the company give us the date of the founding and the names of its officers; the sales ledger reveals the cost of the
product and sales for a specific period; an advertisement in a newspaper may
show us a picture of the product and indicate that it was marketed locally or
even exported, and it might also give its price and tell something about its
use. A specimen of the article gives us an opportunity to assess it for ourselves, to feel it and describe it, to see how it works.

In his 1926 history of my community, Henry Abt deals with a local
industry in the following fashion:

> The Ithaca Glass Works, originally fostered by Ezra Cornell, was established
> in 1874 and reorganized in 1876. The main factory was burned in 1882 and a
> new one, on Third Street between Franklin Street and Railroad Avenue, was
> built in 1883. At the time the new plant was one of the best of its kind in the
> United States. There were five buildings, containing three eight-pot furnaces,
> an engine room, a mill for grinding the crucible material, flattening and an-
> nealing equipment, and cutting and packing departments. Railroads had sid-
> ings at the works. Nine thousand boxes of single and double thick patent white
> crystal sheet glass were shipped over those tracks each month.[2]

This represents the customary treatment of a local industry and provides
excellent details about the factory. Duly footnoted, it easily passed into the
canon of my town's past. This is a typical description. The documents have
led historians in this direction, and we have followed them, willy-nilly. Thus,
by simply surviving, by surfacing from a past era, the documents on which
our business history has been based draw our attention to a particular way of
thinking about this glass factory. We learn about its physicality, its link to
markets, and its product.

This is, however, not all that we want to know about the Ithaca Glass
Works or any other industry. I would like to know who worked for the
company, where they lived, how much they were paid, what sort of compen-
sation they received if hurt on the job, what happened to the workers when
the plant burned, the ethnicity of those who worked there, the social organizations they established for themselves, and the receptiveness of manage-
ment to the creation of a benevolent society or a union. At what age did
workers start in the factory, and were all of the workers male? Did workers'
children attend public schools or the local parochial school, and for how
long? What were the working conditions in the factory, who were the owners, how much money did they take out of the company, and where and how
did they live? If the workers lived near the factory, which I suspect they did,
were there local stores in the neighborhood and did they accept credit? What
happened in the summertime to these local groceries, for glass works did not
produce new ware in the hottest part of the year and many glassworkers
leased houses for only eight months, leaving in the summertime to camp

along the lake. What was the community's attitude about these workers? Were they well regarded? When the company was absorbed by another corporation, which was a common fate in that era of consolidation, what happened to the owners? When the company was abandoned by the parent company in Pittsburgh, what happened to the workers? Did they find other jobs locally, or did they leave the area?

The documents do not provide answers to these questions and little has survived to our day about the workers in the factory or about working conditions, hiring practices, attempts at unionization, crises resulting from pay cuts in times of depression, or even of happy employees well paid for their labors and respected for their craftsmanship. Yet their history is still integral to the story of what happened at the local factory. Few working people wrote letters that have ended up in local historical societies: perhaps those letters were never written; perhaps they were never collected. Without a letter of protest about an unfair firing or letters of complaint from distributors or purchasers about shoddy workmanship, these everyday business episodes have not been written into our history. By ignoring the total story, by not probing for more than partial answers, we allow the surviving documents—and works of earlier local history—to shape the history we tell. This leads to an incomplete history. Workers made the product, merchants offered it for sale, and someone bought it. These are all aspects of the history of the company, but only infrequently are these various persons or viewpoints mentioned in business documents, and thus they are rarely part of the history we know.

I once met a woman who was writing the history of a small cheese factory. She knew who had founded the company and how it operated; she could explain the entire process necessary to produce various cheeses offered for sale; and she knew with some accuracy the area in which the cheese was distributed. However, because the documents did not mention the people who worked in the factory, she never thought about them as an obvious part of her study, and she was startled when I asked about them. They were, she muttered to me, "just local women."

"Aha," says the women's historian, or the labor historian, with great eagerness. But no, insisted this local historian, workers were not important because they only "came in part-time and there is no record of them." The documents we use can reveal to us only what they were designed to record. It is up to the local historian to form questions that will unveil a more complete picture of the past, a past that is more complex—and often more interesting—than we will ever know if we accept at face value only that which ends up on our desks or in an archive.

If we are really interested in finding out more about the glass plant or the cheese factory than what we are given, how do we go about it? After all, workers' letters are rarely found in local archives, and employers' reactions to strikes are not necessarily part of the business documents stashed away in the local historical society. Where, then, do we look? How do we find out what we want to know, rather than merely what the extant documents readily tell us?

In the first place, there are newspapers—and often their articles reflect more diverse information than other sources. For example, none of the documents about the glass works mentions labor unrest, but the following short notice appeared in a local newspaper: "A few days ago a number of blowers at the Ithaca Glass Works were dismissed to make room for new men. The discharged workmen made some threats and the police were called upon to protect the property. No hostile demonstration has as yet, however, been made."[3] Newspaper research is most rewarding, but it does take time, and only a few local newspapers are indexed, though some today are searchable if they have been digitized—a great boon to local researchers. I wish my local paper were available in a digital form. Now, through the miracles of technology, my local newspaper is currently being digitized. I am very conscious how this will change research questions, thoroughness, and completeness of local history topics.

Information in newspapers is often only part of the story. The problem I find is that newspapers whet my interest about something but the supporting information is often not to be found. For example, there was never any other mention of the men from the glass factory displaced by new workers, so I do not know why this happened or where the old employees went—if they found other jobs locally or if they left the community. I do not know if they received some aid from the factory, from the community, or from their churches. The story, unfortunately in this case, and so often in local history efforts, runs out.

Another approach is to look through city directories (in which a person's occupation is often listed along with an indication of home ownership) and seek out the manuscript census—presently available at the federal level up to 1940 except for the lost records of 1890—in order to locate workers by occupation and by place of residence. Using both sources of information is most helpful because the city directory, an annual production in many locales, will reveal sequential occupations that the decennial census cannot show. The city directory may also reveal occupational clusters and individual changes of residence, something that is interesting to track when a renter shifts from place to place or when a homeowner sells one house and moves to another. This information begins to reveal a broader view of the factory and its workers, and it may offer unforeseen rewards. Workers' names, ages, and marital status and the value of their real estate—information often found in the manuscript census sheets—help build a more comprehensive portrait. Church records may corroborate this census information and provide death dates as well, information that will allow an obituary search in local newspapers. Wills or inventories might be located. Physical evidence can also be sought: houses built for the workers often still stand; cemetery records and family gravestones are often extant; and we can sometimes come across a communal memory of a factory and its employees. A photograph might have been taken at a company picnic, or a local newspaper might list company employees who participated in a special excursion. Taken together, all these bits of evidence help us create a fuller picture of what went on in the factory and who worked there. Look also at the consequences of a plant closing: Do workers disappear from the local records? Do some remain to find other employment? Items with dates send us scurrying back to newspaper morgues—if they exist—and the past becomes more and more complex. Most of what will be discovered will be about the factory, owners, and products, but it is important that we attempt to put the workers into the picture as best we can.

Can we also draw parallel pictures of employers and employees and find those places where they interacted, where the two groups met: picnics, strikes, church? Our story becomes richer, and gradually the past yields its secrets. Frequently we cannot answer all the questions we pose about a subject, but one of the delights of pursuing local history is that, at this microscopic level, we can often find more than might be expected.

Table 6.1.

Andrews, William R.	glass factory	51 Esty Street
Andris, Gustave	glass factory	70 Willow Ave.
Arc, Gregory	glass factory	23 Auburn St.
Arc, Joseph	glass factory	23 Auburn St.
Ballsizer, Valentine	glass factory	Hancock & Third
Barker, Charles	glass factory	47 N. Fulton
Barrett, Howard	glass factory	b. 81 Cascadilla St.
Baur, Joseph	glass factory	44 W. Mill
Bean, William	glass factory	b. 34 Hancock
Bertram, Adolf	glass factory	48 Hancock
Bierbrauer, George	glass factory	b. 10 Lake Ave.
Boland, James	glass factory	b. 6 Lewis St.

This is not easy research to pursue, and it does not always tell us what we want to know, but by attempting it we have a chance to create a fuller reconstruction of the past. We can follow up on the glassworkers by looking at the *Ithaca City Directory*, in which residents of the city are listed in alphabetical order.[4] Without knowing the names of the workers, of course, we cannot look them up, but we can scan through the occupations listed for entrants and create our own list. Once we have names, we can see which other family members are listed (as most adults were in the 1880s for my community), and we can plot their places of residence on a local map. Table 6.1 shows some of the city directory entries for the As and Bs; the letter b before an address indicates that the individual boarded and was not a home owner. What is immediately interesting in this list, of course, is the number of workers who owned their own homes.

In all, there are 119 workers listed for the two glass companies in town, plus M. H. Heagany, the superintendent of one of the factories. Divided in half, that would mean that each factory employed approximately sixty people. I do not know, however, if the companies were exactly the same size; one might have been larger than the other and, therefore, might have had a slightly larger workforce. Many of the workers have names that might indicate they were born elsewhere, but relatively few are Irish—an interesting fact, because a substantial number of Irish settled in this community during the 1840s and 1850s but they seem to have adopted other occupations. One of those on the master list is surely a woman, most likely the secretary to the company president; another person might be female, although the name is no firm clue.[5]

What do we learn from this exercise? If we chart the residences of these workers, we find them clustered in two sections of the community, both adjacent to the factories. Only one man of those listed had a long, and potentially difficult, walk to work. He lived two and a half miles away on South Hill, and in bad weather he would have had an uncomfortable trip to either factory but in 1884 a trolley line opened that might have made his trip, at two cents each way, easier. If we then take these 120 names and group them by the streets on which they lived, we can go next to the state manuscript census for 1885 or the federal census for 1900, locate those streets, and track down even more information.

From the census, we can determine the number of resident aliens working in the glass industry; we can find out how long they had been in the community; we can learn their ages, whether they owned their own homes or rented, and if they were literate; and we can learn about their dependents and if minor children in the family were attending school. An interesting side note emerges from this material: although many of the community's laborers who are listed in the city directory had wives who worked as domestics around the town, not one glassworker listed a female—wife, mother, or daughter—who did such work. This suggests that salaries in the glass factories were adequate to support a family. The census, by listing individuals' occupations and the value of homes, can help us determine if this general impression is true. Neither the city directory nor the census is absolutely infallible, but research in them can help us draw an interesting group picture of people so often neglected in our local history. So, too, can Sanborn Fire Insurance maps, those useful and detailed area maps, if they are available for your community.[6]

Of the 119 glassworkers there are at least eight cases in which we can locate more than three members of a family sharing this same occupation. This may suggest that those individuals felt that employment at the glass factory supplied them with enough money to meet their needs and that they encouraged other family members to join them. If the pay had been poor, or if working conditions were intolerable, it is unlikely that a man would willingly bring his sons and brothers into the factory, though in many cases even disagreeable or dangerous work was welcome when other opportunities were not available.

Documentary material for any community is usually incomplete. The next diary in a sequence telling of a woman's struggle with her religious beliefs, the key letter of a series from a soldier on San Juan Hill, or a bank account book that would allow the researcher to understand a particular failure is invariably the missing link. So, too, the senior citizen who lived through a special event always seems to have died the week before a historical investigation begins. How many times have you heard: "You should have been here last month when Mrs. Evans could have told you everything. But she just died." Even if these crucial pieces of evidence were available, would we be able to understand the past fully?

Probably not. A soldier on a battlefield can only report on the action of his platoon or the small group of buddies in the foxhole with him. His view from over the rim is limited and he does not know about the battle down the line or in the next woods. A minister can only give us his view of a church schism; even if he understands the reasons why the parishioners on the other side oppose him, he is not always the best witness to their concerns. A father can only tell us his version of his son's decision to seek his fortune elsewhere—and even if he can empathize with his son's wanderlust or desire for greater gain, his understanding is affected by his own love and desire that his child be safe and nearby. Our evidence is skewed right from the start; we must always seek its internal bias even before we accept its testimony. Understanding that, we can go on to ask questions of the materials we have and extend our knowledge of the past beyond the limitations of our documents. Our questions about past events, about prior institutions, traditions, and habits, should never be limited by what is apparently available. As grateful as we should be for documents that survive, we must always feel dissatisfied with the documents we use, so that we do not simply accept what is given but, rather, seek for all that may be of interest.

There is no rule or set of rules that tells us when we have looked far and long enough, or searched fully, or asked enough questions to feel certain that what we say is correct or that our search is done. Many historians would prefer to have at least two pieces of independent evidence to be assured of any fact. Being absolutely sure about the past, believing in your accuracy, depends on several things. The first is thorough research, the second is general knowledge of the area and the period, and the third is contemporary knowledge or judgment about the place you are describing and about human nature. But there is a fourth ingredient in this process of knowing—and that is an imaginative, intuitive response to the past based on knowledge of place and time and the questions we ask about it. What is the point of the work on the glass factory: partly we research the topic to know what went on in that abandoned building, who created those bottles or clocks or jugs, what impact that had on the community in terms of local sales and products shipped elsewhere. But knowing specifics, which is what the public expects of historians, is one things. Knowing them to say something about the community is another. What the presence of the glass factories says about my community is varied: that they appeared when transportation was fairly good from this rather isolated place; that local men invested locally, keeping funds active in our community is another—rather than sending money created here elsewhere, such as investing in western lands, or in stocks in a company in another location. Other things we can observe is that these workers came to our city for work rather than being drawn from the current population—and that says something about mobility, about the importance of employment opportunities, and it tells us another thing: none of the names of the glassworkers come from the local, small but growing African American community. So the glass factories probably attracted skilled labor; they were paid fairly well. But the factories did not last as the era of consolidation meant that in less than a decade they were gone from our community. Did the workers remain? I don't know, but it is certainly a question to follow up.

There are always questions. Some are obvious, others less so. In Ithaca in 1823, citizens banded together to found an academy.[7] That is a fact. About the academy there is a good deal of information. I know the people who were involved in the venture, who contributed to it, what the newspaper thought about it, the hopes community members held out for it, and the benefits they believed that they would reap. I have notices of the opening of classes, the cost, and the subjects to be studied. I know the names and backgrounds of many of the teachers, and I have several end-of-year catalogs that list the students, their courses of study, and their grades.

I know a great deal about the community and about the traditions from which these people came. There is one thing, however, that I do not know from the available information, and that is why this small academy in this central New York village admitted both boys and girls. Single-sex academies were the norm throughout New England; even in central New York, in the larger towns and nascent cities along the major route west, academies were ordinarily segregated by gender. Yet in Ithaca and in some of the smaller communities south of the Great Western Road we find coeducational institutions—at a time when many learned people believed that too much education was detrimental to the development of females and that males and females should not be educated together. Why, then, in the 1820s in Ithaca, Homer, Cortland, and Moravia were the schools coeducational?

There is nothing written in the sources that answers this question, and yet I think I know the answer. I know it because of my work in the primary sources, because of general knowledge, and because of my understanding of what sort of place this small village was. I know it also because of what I think I know about people in general. My speculation is that in communities such as Ithaca and Homer, where there was a tiny population, there were probably too few families with enough wealth to maintain two academies— one for boys and one for girls. So only one was built, and those who were able to educate their children sent boys and girls to the same building. In that schoolhouse, the boys had one entrance, the girls had another, and the primary classes were segregated. The upper-level courses, however—where there were but four or five students to take mathematics or Latin—were open to any student academically prepared to enroll in them.

I am fairly certain that the size of the village and the economics of one institution rather than two provide an answer to the question of why our particular academy taught both boys and girls. But I cannot footnote such an assertion, and I certainly cannot prove it. Knowing history depends on a great many things, and knowing with real certainty will not happen all that often.

In an earlier edition of this book I included a discussion of types of documents a local historian is likely to encounter, along with comments about the problems inherent in those documents and the possibilities they might present. My comments were drawn from my own experience as a local historian and filled with what I hoped were "wise" words. This section is somewhat harder—or easier, depending on one's outlook—to write today. It is harder and easier for the same reason, and that is that there are now other books to which I can readily send the reader that take up the discussion of sources for local history in a thorough, if not such a personal, way.

Nearby History: Exploring the Past around You, published by AltaMira Press and the American Association for State and Local History (AASLH), is now available in a third edition dated 2010.[8] This book, put together by David E. Kyvig and Myron A. Marty, sets out to address "the gulf between academic, nationally oriented history, and nonacademic, locally oriented history." The book is chock-full of references to historical guides, subjects, and methods of doing history. I find the specialized books in the series that followed *Nearby History* particularly helpful for historians interested in the history of houses, church or educational history, banks, and other aspects of community life.

The second book is the *Encyclopedia of Local History*, also published by AltaMira and AASLH.[9] The first edition was published in 2000, and my friend Norma Prendergast and I edited the book. The second edition appeared in 2012, and Amy H. Wilson was my coeditor. In this book, there are essays about sources historians can expect to find and those sources that local historians should seek out, including commentary on newspapers, diaries, letters, the federal census, photographs, and other documents. There are essays about ways of doing history that note the classic books in each field, essays about social, economic, western, women's, children's, family, public, and architectural history. There are also articles about local history as it is practiced around the world (New Zealand, Scotland, England, Canada, and more). Other essays discuss various fields of history that pertain to the doing of local history and in them writers answer questions most frequently asked about that field, and also to identify those questions that people do not necessarily know enough to ask. I recommend that you find a copy of the *Encyclopedia*, open it to something that interests you, and then browse about in it to see what else you might find. It is loaded with wisdom, good advice, and good humor.

With these two books, local historians can look up what they need to know about the mechanics of doing local history. Once research has been undertaken, *Writing Local History Today: A Guide to Researching, Publishing, and Marketing Your Book*, by Thomas A. Mason and J. Kent Calder (also published by AltaMira Press, 2013) is invaluable.[10]

THE ANTI-INDEX

I am sometimes asked why we need another biography of Abraham Lincoln, or—and not in the same league—why we need a new local history. My hometown has had three written histories prior to the publication of my history of the county in 1985. Two of these earlier books were collections of short articles on various aspects of the past compiled in the nineteenth century and are county histories of the standard type. Both of these earlier volumes contain information of great use to me, although there are no footnotes. These volumes focus on the development of the area, its leading citizens, and its civic advancement: that is, the creation of churches, the establishment of schools, and the purification of water. The third book is a city history printed in 1926, again without footnotes, although it does contain a bibliography. The thrust of this last history is the development of local institutions, such as churches, businesses, and voluntary organizations; the origins of manufacturing establishments; products made locally; good works in the community; and fraternal and church organizations. Its interests mirror those of the 1920s.[11]

Each history amplifies earlier books, each adds to the canon, and each reflects its own time and author—even if that was a committee or an agent, or a local historian working on his own. We learn more about Lincoln with each book but we also gain new perspectives on his life and achievements with each author's interest and abilities. With local history, each new rendering amplifies the past and reflects present concerns.

In my local history books, and in some others in my library, I keep an "anti-index"; that is, on the inside back cover of those books I write in the topics that I sought within them but could not find. This is not a list of charges or sins of omission committed by those earlier authors. I am not faulting them for not writing about women or the environment. Rather, my anti-index works in a positive way to enhance my understanding of my own historical interests and the interests of my own time. When I review the topics that I have written down, I can see themes emerge, and I discover in the pattern of entries subjects that concerned me and the topics about which earlier authors had no interest whatsoever. The anti-index helps me nail down shifts in our thinking about place.

For example, on the back cover of the 1926 history of my town the following items not included in the book are listed:

Rulloff–Clark
crime
influx of the Irish in 1830s
American Party—Know Nothings
cigar workers
OAU
Copperhead sympathy during the Civil War
Inlet Mission
Italians/Greeks
Notable women and Suffrage
Immaculate Conception (Roman Catholic) Church
Roorback
Tailor's Strike

This is not a complete list, but the items give some idea of what I looked for in the book and could not find. I can group the list by categories of interest that really do reflect my, and history's, more current interests:

- Ethnicity accounts for a number of entries, such as the Irish and other foreign-born, and the OAU—the Order of the American Union, a nativist organization of the 1870s and 1880s was devoted to keeping Roman Catholics out of political power.[12]
- Notable local women: Samantha Nivison wanted to establish a water-cure hospital that would train women to become doctors; Shawanebeke (or Mrs. Benchley) agitated for women's suffrage and was regarded as a local crank, though today I think of her fondly for her causes and ardor which

mirror my own. Grace Miller White was a novelist remembered for her book *Tess of the Storm Country*, twice made into a movie. [13]

- Deviance is another category. Under it we find Rulloff, a notorious murderer, and Guy Clark, who axed his wife to death in 1832. [14] Political deviance would account for the Copperheads, or northern Democrats, prevalent in the area during the Civil War but never mentioned by any of our local historians, yet the evidence is that there were plenty of them that could be found around "this neck of the woods."
- History of work covers a number of entries. Cigar workers were mostly women and children; men sold (and smoked) stogies, but women and children made and boxed them. The cigar workers staged at least one strike in Ithaca, as did the tailors. [15]

While the past does not change, our historical interests do. My anti-index allows me to chart the historical fashions of my own time, just as I look in older histories to see what the historical style or angle was in times past. We can look in our older histories for their time's fashions and historical questions, and thus we have yet another way of understanding those who have gone before us. We write the history of a community by asking questions that interest us today. We discover that our views of the past differ from the views of previous writers—people who were, after all, writing about the same place and with much of the same evidence available today. Yet our books are different; and so they should be, for 1894 is not 2014, and we have learned a great deal and changed greatly in terms of our interests and concerns. Simply to repeat the history of the past by reprinting it or recycling it is a great waste of human effort and resources. It is also to deny the present, to imply that it is not as interesting or important as early times—which of course is not true. We and our contemporary audience deserve better than to perpetuate the bias of the past. Our attitudes today about many things are more tolerant, more accepting than those of earlier days. The history we write should reflect our own era. The future will, as it always does, find enough to complain about—we need not add to our own misadventures the outmoded attitudes and ethos of another time.

TAKE NOTE

What about credit? When writing local history, what about the debts we owe to authors who have written on our topic—those who have informed us or those with whom we disagree? Footnotes tell the reader where we have been, what we have looked at, and why we have reached particular conclusions. Footnotes give credit to those who know more than we do about a particular subject, those from whom we have learned, and those who have advanced ideas that we have borrowed because those ideas help illuminate what we are working on. Footnotes are a map showing how we came to view the past in a particular way, they tell the reader who first said something, and they lead a reader or another researcher to additional information about a subject. Without footnotes, our work cannot be checked, and it will be less useful to others. With good or even adequate footnotes, we can take our place in the chain of human knowing—not at all a bad place to be.

Unhelpful footnotes are those that are incomplete, inaccurate, or misleading. They send readers to the wrong volume, refer to the wrong page, cite an author with incorrect initials, or lack critical information. Examples of these horrors abound. There is nothing mysterious, however, about a footnote. It is a pledge to readers and to later historians that what is written is based on evidence that can be consulted by others. A scientist publishes his or her laboratory method and results so that other researchers can replicate the experiment and go on to new investigations. For historians, footnotes serve a similar purpose.

I once worked with an elderly man on a pamphlet-sized history. When I presented the text to him, he looked at the footnotes interspersed throughout and sputtered: "No footnotes." He believed that the historian's aim was to be read, and, being a retired printer, he wanted to sell books. He feared anything that would put off the readers. "Footnotes will scare 'em away," he repeated to me at least twice weekly. The reader does not care where you got it, he believed; the reader just wants to enjoy it. "And," he bellowed at me, "I want him to enjoy it too."

I could never convince my friend to use footnotes, and our joint effort contains none. But I was wrong to give up the fight. Footnotes need not intimidate readers, who can easily bypass those little numbers and easily ignore endnotes included at the back of a book. The absence of footnotes, however, places a book in limbo. Unfootnoted books are not useful as history because we have no way of knowing how those authors gathered their information or if the books were written from "common knowledge." (Nor are such books folklore, for they lack the methodology necessary in that discipline as well.)

Henry Charlton Beck, the author of a number of popular and unfootnoted books about legends of New Jersey, complains in *More Forgotten Towns of Southern New Jersey* about the patronizing treatment his books received from academic historians. Beck's books were placed in one library where it was the policy to loan books of nonfiction freely but to charge the reader for fiction. A critic of Beck's style and lack of method borrowed one of his earliest books from the library and returned it with utmost speed. Beck reported that with some ostentation he placed the book before the librarian and handed over a fee. The librarian protested that there was no charge for nonfiction; but the indignant reader snorted, "My money says what it is," and out he stormed.[16] My elderly friend and Beck had similar attitudes about history. Both came into the field from the newspaper world; both were interested in telling a good story, in attracting and keeping readers; and both were rather successful at doing just that. They gathered their information where they could and from whoever had a tale to tell. They repeated what they heard in such a way as to amuse and entertain. Neither man was concerned about the study of history or about the need for one generation of historians to be accountable to the next. They were in fact, more interested in selling books than adding to a community's culture or knowledge of itself.

What we write about our communities will be looked at in the future by people who want to write about America's hometowns, and the problem with unfootnoted history is that it presents a dead end to those who want to know how we know. If we offer no indication to future historians as to how or where information was gathered, and if there is no way for readers to check on a statement that interests them, then our work will not stand the test of time even if what we have to say is valuable.

What should a footnote say? We local historians are not writing academic dissertations, and our footnotes need not be tomes of argument. They should be simple and to the point. A good footnote tells the reader who first said a thing, on what on piece of evidence or several pieces of information an opinion has been based, and what gives a writer the authority to move an argument forward from one point to another. A good footnote contains specific information showing how a statement can be made and where evidence can be found. It should tell in what letter, located in which collection, and in what archive we will find a quotation. It should state in which book, with what title, published when and where, and on what page we can discover a similar or dissimilar argument. A footnote should allow us to unpeel a work of local history to see how the layers were built up, thereby creating the whole.

Footnotes for works of local history can be written in many styles, but simplicity might be the best rule. When quoting a letter written by Calista Hall, a historian simply states the following:

> Calista Hall to Pliny Hall, 16 August 1849, in the Smelzer Collection, Department of Manuscripts and University Archives, Cornell University.

When crediting something from a diary, the notation might read:

> Belle Cowdry Diary, 6 February 1857, 28, DeWitt Historical Society of Tompkins County [now called The History Center], Ithaca, NY.

These citations show that the material quoted, or the source that gives a reason to assert something, can be found in these places. Readers interested in seeing the quotation in its original context or reviewing its collateral information can write or visit these repositories and judge for themselves how the original information supports that which was footnoted.

The use of a footnote requires some judgment. Where there are several references to be footnoted in one paragraph, they may be clustered together into one note, the number appearing at the end of the text. They should be listed in the order of their appearance in the paragraph. All other footnotes follow these basic forms:

> Calista Hall[writer] to Pliny Hall [receiver of letter], 16 August 1849, in Carl N. Degler, *At Odds: Women and the Family in America from the Revolution to the Present* (New York: Oxford University Press, 1980), 211. [This is a book that quotes the letter.]

Or

> Carol Kammen, ed., "The Letters of Calista Hall," *New York History* 43 (April 1982): 209–34. [This sends the reader to a published form of the letter, from which Carl Degler quoted and cites the location of the original.]

If citing the original, the note would read:

> Smelzer Family Papers. 1811-1941, #1184, Kroch Library, Rare and Manu-scripts, Cornell University Library, Ithaca, NY.

In each case, the footnote tells us where the quotation or the information can be found.

Other footnotes expand on these basic formulas by adding the number of the volume when quoting something that has appeared in a series (a serial is a magazine or periodical, something that is issued sequentially or in a series) or adding other useful information that will help the reader locate the source. If Calista Hall's letters were still in private hands, as is much of the material that local historians use, the footnote might state: "Calista Hall to Pliny Hall, 16 August 1849, letter in private collection of Mrs. Nellie Smelzer of Lan-sing, NY." The reader is told to the best of our ability where we found the information used. If we consulted church records, we might note where in the church the records were kept: "Minutes of the Ladies Aid Society, Federated Church, Brooktondale, NY (records kept in the bottom drawer of the histori-cal file in the pastor's study)." While the physical location of privately held records might change, it is helpful to note where they were at the time of use, as sometimes that will give later users a way of tracking them. Records in private hands require us to be as specific as possible about their location at the time the materials were consulted.

There is one particular footnoting problem that most local historians face, and this concerns statements found in our town and county histories. Those books are rarely footnoted themselves, and yet they contain a great deal of material on which local historians depend and which in general, I find to be fairly accurate when I have had occasion to check. To footnote directly to a county history, however, is to lead the reader nowhere in particular, for the writers (or compilers, as many were called) of county histories do not tell us how they knew what they wrote down. To question their source of information is not to question their veracity; but footnoting directly to one of those tomes is not good enough.

My personal rule is to use material in a county history only when I have other source material that corroborates that information. For example, I could not use material in the "Four County History," formally entitled *History of Tioga, Chemung, Tompkins, Schuyler Counties, New York*, published in 1879, to discuss slaves held within the county prior to the 1827 abolition of slavery within the state.[17] I would note that evidence of slavery can be found in census compilations, in which Tompkins County is credited with having ten slaves in 1820. So my footnote would include a citation to the published census figures, reading something like this:

> "Census of the County of Tompkins," *Ithaca Republican Chronicle*, 21 February 1821: 3; "Village of Ithaca," *American Journal* (Ithaca), 24 September 1823: 3; "Census of Ithaca," *The Ithaca Journal*, 5 January 1825: 3; and Census for the State of New York (Albany, 1855), ix.

It may be noted that with primary material leading the reader directly to the source, the inclusion of the county history, in which the mention of slavery is vague at best, is unnecessary.

What of a statement in an unfootnoted town or county history that cannot be verified? If the information is something that I want or need to use, I would then state in the text or in the footnote where the information came from and that I have been unable to verify it elsewhere, but that even while I cannot confirm it, I have no reason to doubt it. Then I use the material as I would any other, and I do not worry about it. Sometimes we have to use our common sense and then move on.

What should be footnoted? There is no firm rule that covers every case, but there are many situations that require us to give credit and some times when it is easy to do so. When someone is quoted directly, a footnote is needed. When an author is quoted indirectly or his or her material is drawn on, credit is needed. When a fact is mentioned that is otherwise unknown or beyond common knowledge, a footnote to the source is needed. For example, it is generally known that once there were slaves within my county, and this fact need not demand a citation. When I categorically state that there were ten slaves, however, it is incumbent on me to tell the reader why I used the number ten rather than twelve or eight. My sources directed me to state ten, and I did so with conviction. I therefore credit my sources.

- A footnote is needed any time an argument is developed that coincides with an argument or disagrees with a contention of another author who has written on a particular subject.
- We need a footnote when something written is a revision of previously held ideas.
- Anytime an author advances knowledge beyond that which was previously known, a footnote is needed.
- When we deviate from that which has been previously stated, we should explain to our readers what evidence induces us to think otherwise.
- If material used is gathered from an individual in an oral interview, that person should be noted or credited in a footnote. An interview with an old-time resident of the area about a flood, or education, or family history might yield useful information. An appropriate footnote will tell who gave you the information used, when you were told, and something about the authority of that individual.

My footnote for a 1935 flood could take one of these forms:

> Conversation, 16 April 2002, with Sally Smith, who was forced from her home by the 1935 flood.

or

> Interview with Paul Smith, 1935 flood survivor, 16 April 2002.

or

> Casual conversation with Paul Smith regarding the 1935 flood, 16 April 2002.

This last form indicates that the information gained from Smith was not the result of a planned interview but, rather, was more informal in nature—in this case, I talked with Smith while I was standing in line at the grocery store.

Footnotes are important, and they are relatively simple to write. They document things other people have said, borrowed ideas, and items that have caused you to think differently. Footnotes should lead to sources, and they also show the transmission of an idea. They lead, sometimes, to more information on a subject. They do not need to scare a reader or a writer.

"But what," a woman asked me some time ago, "do we do when we cannot footnote our material?" She added that in some instances footnotes would be expensive to add to a text and in other instances they would be inappropriate. Footnotes often add to the cost of printing if they are placed at the bottom of the page, but as endnotes following a chapter or at the end of a book they add little to the overall cost: "When are they inappropriate?" I asked. The woman replied: "In a church bulletin that might carry a historical announcement, on a poster, perhaps, or souvenir pieces issued by a community. What then should be done?"

It seems to me that there are two solutions to this problem. The first is to take one copy of the text, whatever it might be, annotate it with references, and place this special copy in the nearest archive. This annotation can be done on the page itself or on an accompanying sheet of paper; or if extra pages are sewn in the book, then the footnotes can be written on the interleaved sheets.

The second solution is what I call the "sneaky" footnote. This is a way of footnoting material that usually does not receive such careful treatment. A writer of local history in the public press is someone who is faced with the problem of giving credit in a medium in which editors and others would frown on and most likely delete the insertion of a real footnote. The sneaky footnote is better than nothing. Information, or as much of it as possible, can be written directly into the text. It usually does little for the graceful flow of the article, but it does manage to give credit where credit is due, and it directs readers to the appropriate source.

"As Calista Hall wrote to her husband, on 16 August 1849, in a letter donated by Nellie Smelzer to the Cornell Archives" is one way to begin a statement and give credit at the same time. Another way is to introduce a fact by noting that it "appears in the section on the Town of Caroline in the 'Four County History,'" and still another is to note that historian Carl Degler quotes Calista Hall in his 1980 book *At Odds.*

In each case, there is enough information to get an interested reader to the right archive, where the index of holdings will lead to the letter in question, or to the author's name and book title. There is enough information to be helpful but not too much apparatus to put off an editor, who is likely to regard footnotes as pedantic and antithetical to his or her idea of what should appear in a newspaper.

It is particularly important that local historians be conscientious about footnotes because often the materials with which we deal are outside common repositories and, therefore, are unknown to others. Our footnotes do more than reveal our sources; through them we share knowledge of local materials with others engaged in similar or related studies. We also show the usefulness of materials in private hands that might seem to their owners to have little general historical value.

By writing accurate footnotes, by annotating special copies of publications that are not to be footnoted, and by inserting a sneaky footnote into material not generally dealt with in this way, we local historians keep faith with those on whom we leaned—and from whom we learned—and we keep faith with those who will come after, offering our footnotes as a token of openness and honesty, one generation to another. Our responsibility, I believe, is to "leave footnotes unto others as we would have footnotes left unto us." If this sounds like a hard-and-fast rule, so be it. Consider how much easier our task would be today if the historians who preceded us had followed that rule. I can think of no more important dictum for local historians to follow. It keeps us honest, and it is our link of trust with the future.

Leave footnotes unto others as we would have footnotes left unto us.

TAKING NOTE

All this leaves us with one final topic to consider, and that is the issue of note taking, for it is on the quality of the notes we take when researching that we write our footnotes. There are people with hard-and-fast rules about 3 x 5 cards for bibliographic citations and 5 x 8 pads for information, whereas others prefer different sizes and even different colors of paper to distinguish among various archives. With computers, people devise their own systems that identify gathered information. My friends all seem to use Note Bene but there are other programs as well that track footnotes for a writer.

In essence, what is important is that every piece of information you take down be keyed to its source so you can state in a footnote that a particular fact or stress can be found on a certain page in a particular book, or in an archival collection, or on a map located in a map collection. I try to record all this information in such a way that I have all the details I need when I go to write. Human nature being what it is, or my habits being what they are, I sometimes fail to get everything necessary for writing a complete note, which means that I then have to retrace my own path back through the library to relocate a page number or date. Doing this once or twice should be enough to alert us to the tortures of backtracking, and it should be enough to make us careful at the outset that we retrieve what we know we will need. Going back and checking twice is simply a way of life for many historians, but taking complete citation notes at the outset is a great favor to yourself.

NOTES

1. "An Address, Delivered before the New Hampshire Historical Society, at the Annual Meeting, 11th June 1828," in *Collections of the New Hampshire Historical Society* (1832): 125 and reprinted in *Pursuit of Local History* (Walnut Creek, CA: AltaMira Press, 1996), 61–65.

2. Henry Abt, *Ithaca* (Ithaca: Ross W. Kellogg Publisher, 1926), 117.

3. *The Ithaca Democrat*, December 27, 1883.

4. Henry Mente, canvasser and compiler, *Ithaca General and Business Directory for 1884–85* (Ithaca: Norton and Conklin, 1885).

5. See Graham Hodges, "History of Work," in *Encyclopedia of Local History*, ed. Carol Kammen and Norma Prendergast (Walnut Creek, CA: AltaMira Press, 2000), 478–86.

6. See Ed Salo, "Sanborn Fire Insurance Maps," in *Encyclopedia of Local History*, 402; and see the Library of Congress, *Union Lists of Sanborn Fire Insurance Maps Held by Institutions in the United States and Canada*—microfilm copies may be purchased from the Library of Congress Photoduplication Service and from the D. A. Sanborn Fire Insurance Company, 629 Fifth Avenue, Pelham, NY 10803; 914-738-1649; www.sanborn.map.com.

7. See M. Teresa Baer, "History of Education," in *Encyclopedia of Local History*, 146–48.

8. David E. Kyvig and Myron A. Marty, eds., *Nearby History: Exploring the Past around You* (Lanham, MD: AltaMira Press, 2010).

9. Carol Kammen and Amy H. Wilson, *Encyclopedia of Local History*, 2nd ed. (Lanham, MD: AltaMira Press, 2012).

10. Thomas A. Mason and J. Kent Calder, *Writing Local History Today: A Guide to Researching, Publishing, and Marketing Your Book* (Lanham, MD: AltaMira Press, 2013).

11. D. H. H., *History of Tioga, Chemung, Tompkins, and Schuyler Counties, New York* (Philadelphia: Everts and Ensign, 1879); John H. Selkreg, ed., *Landmarks of Tompkins County, New York* (Syracuse: D. Mason and Co., 1894); and Abt, *Ithaca*.

12. See John Bodnar, "Ethnicity" and "Nativism," in *Encyclopedia of Local History*, 166–68, 340.

13. See Marsha Semmel, "Women's History," in *Encyclopedia of Local History*, 474–76; and Mary Beth Norton, "Women's Legal Status," in *Encyclopedia of Local History*, 477–78.

14. See Theresa Lehr, "History of Crime," in *Encyclopedia of Local History*, 127–30.

15. See Hodges, "History of Work," and Patrizia Sione and Richard Strassberg, "Labor History," in *Encyclopedia of Local History*, 272–77.

16. Henry Charlton Beck, *More Forgotten Towns of Southern New Jersey* (New Brunswick, NJ: Quinn and Boden, 1963), 5–6.

17. D. H. H., *History of Tioga, Chemung, Tompkins, and Schuyler Counties, New York*, 458.

Coda to Chapter 6

When Being Right Is Not Good Enough

Like many of you, I am frequently asked to review how other people use local history. I am happy to read drafts—rough and otherwise—in the belief that the more eyes that see a work before it is "carved in stone," the better.

A while ago a publisher sent me a manuscript made up of short biographical sketches of famous people linked to particular places. No sources were given as the basis for the essays, and the information seemed to have been gathered from general biographical dictionaries and encyclopedias. To start with, I was not overly impressed. But I was only a reader, not a publisher putting up money to produce this book, and I am certainly not the best judge of what will sell.

On the whole, most of the information was probably correct. I did not read and fact-check each entry, as that is not what had been asked of me. But I carefully read the biographical sketches of people about whom I have written or done some research. While few things in those pages were actually wrong, there was a great deal that was not quite right—that just would not do. The author used material without giving any thought to balance, nor had information been used with any sort of judiciousness. Let me give several examples of the problem:

- The author implies that John C. Frémont opened up 25 percent of our country, a statement that is inaccurate and goes against the grain of much current thought about western expansion. I can hear Professor Patricia Limerick say, "Opened up to whom?" and "Single-handedly?" Yeah. We can probably all agree that the western part of this country was not actually closed and that it was certainly not empty. In addition, Frémont went west as the leader of a group of men who followed him through thick and thin, and often it was very thin. I think of Herr Preuss, who complained bitterly just about every step he took in his travels with Frémont. So this statement gave me pause.

- Or, again from the Frémont selection, it is implied that he personally received the Mexican surrender of California at Cahuenga on January 13, 1847. Well, yes, Captain Frémont did officiate at the surrender. The statement is not factually false—but it is inadequate and misleading, for Frémont received the surrender *despite* the fact that he had no orders from his superiors to do so and, in fact, had been told not to; in addition, and this is crucial, he faced a court-martial for his actions that day and thereafter. So although Frémont did receive the Mexican surrender (a true statement), he was reprimanded for doing so, which should certainly qualify that particular fact.

- Elizabeth Cady Stanton is linked to the National Women's Hall of Fame, a museum the author describes in detail. And, indeed, Stanton is honored there. But the facts that her house in Seneca Falls is open to the public, that the Women's Rights National Historic Park is just down the street from the Hall of Fame, and that the Seneca County Historical Society as well as the Library of Congress hold important artifacts marking the actions of Stanton and others involved with the 1848 Women's Rights Convention are totally ignored. So, yes, it is true that she is honored in the National Women's Hall of Fame, but that is only a single place in Seneca Falls where she is remembered. The statement is true but incomplete.

At the same time I was reading this manuscript I encountered an essay in *The New Yorker* by Daniel Kevles, a historian of science at Yale University. Kevles writes: "He seemed not to know that errors vary in their scientific significance, that evaluating their meaning involves critical judgment, and that discrimination in the use of data is a feature of scientific inquiry."[1] Much the same could be said of historical inquiry; research is not a matter of copying information from secondary sources—even if that information is in itself correct. And those people who skim off the "interesting parts" of history should certainly not give the public half-truths, or partial truths, or facts that do not tell the truth. The work of the historian involves evaluation, organization, and critical judgment, knowledge of context, discrimination, and thoughtfulness.

The second episode that made me think about half-truth occurred when I received a list of citations for new historical markers that had been approved by a nearby town and sent off to a foundry—which is as close to "carved in stone" as one can get. I was asked if there were any significant events that had been missed because there was money for additional markers. As any of you who have created the text for a historical marker know, whatever the subject, writing in limited space is extremely difficult. In the text I reviewed, compression had created some odd grammatical problems and some offensive abbreviations that I was sure people in the area would not appreciate. There was also a problem with the selection of particular words, some of which were simply incorrect, others of which were historically misused, and still others of which were misleading.

There were, moreover, two general problems. The first was similar to that encountered in the book project. Compression had created partial truths by imparting a fragment of the story while skirting the real significance of the place being marked. In the process, things not true, and probably not even intended to be read as true, were clearly implied. Statements were not exactly wrong, but they certainly were not right either.

The second problem was even more difficult to explain and correct. I spoke with a member of the town board who did not care about interpretation, shadings of meaning, or even the choice of what was being commemorated—some of which was highly questionable—as long as there was nothing on these historical markers that could be proved to be "factually wrong." Yet, while most of what was written was not exactly wrong, much seemed unimportant, trivial, or outdated in its emphasis. In one case, an early railroad was commemorated, yet the fact that this was a horse-drawn line rather than a steam-powered engine was totally ignored. The signs also copied the patterns of those erected in the 1930s by naming first families, first supervisors, first mills, and other initial events—as if after its period of settlement, history in the area stopped. None, for instance, commemorated anything that had happened in the twentieth century. The implication here is fairly clear: only initial events are important.

Every piece of information about the past is not worthy of commemoration. We need to know all we can; but knowing, we make judgments. We must learn what is significant instead of using whatever has been found simply because it is old. Being a historian involves more than just knowing "old stuff"—or even knowing where to find facts. Being a historian and using history—especially on behalf of the public—depends on a delicate balance between the meaning of what is known and what is not known, placed in a carefully understood context.

Any historian asked to write historical markers or to create short biographies of famous people would begin with a question about why the material was wanted in the first place and to what use this history was being put. Historical markers are intended to help a particular place promote a sense of itself by the use of history. That is okay with me. But then the next question must be, what sense of itself? Should they recall old elite families, the first on the land, people who did something significant? What are the criteria for being remembered or remarked upon?

In addition, historical markers should be easy to read; they should give a sense of what happened, communicate the significance of the site, and explain the events or people being commemorated. Certainly, short biographies are difficult to write. But difficulty is not reason enough to slant the truth or to ignore what is unattractive or quirky about people of the past. Fragments of the truth distort the meaning of what we are trying to convey. Shouldn't these projects reflect some of the diversity of the past, some of the humor of the human situation, some of the changes that created problems or opened up opportunities?

Doing history can appear to be deceptively simple. It does not require arcane language or technical training. But it does demand that the historian do more than simply locate facts and copy them from one place to another. History is about the questions we ask, the purposes to which we put information, and it is about careful investigation, balance, discretion, thoughtfulness, fairness, context, and, finally, clear communication. We must stand up for the fact that being right is not good enough.

In response to an earlier form of this essay, Dwight Pitcaithley, the chief historian of the National Park Service, sent me a delightful note he had received. It is worth reprinting, and I do so here with the permission of Constantine J. Dillon, National Park Service superintendent of Fire Island National Seashore, who wrote:

> Well, shoot, I've spent a lot of time preparing a terse, yet not wrong text. Are you now suggesting that these should not be used?
>
> • ABRAHAM LINCOLN: President of the United States 1861–1865. No significant accomplishments after leaving office.
> • SANTA FE TRAIL: Popular route used by people to travel through the Midwest in the 1840s.
> • CORNELIUS VANDERBILT: Though among the richest people in America, he never owned his own car or watched television.
> • FRANKLIN ROOSEVELT: Man who is pictured on the dime.
> • AMERICAN INDIANS: Native people of North America whose numbers have declined sharply over the past 400 years.
> • 14TH AMENDMENT: Constitutional amendment coming after the 13th amendment but before the 15th amendment.
> • APOLLO 11: Space flight that took place in 1969.
> • TITANIC: One of the largest ocean liners ever built. Only used once.

NOTE

1. Daniel Kevles, "Annals of Science: The Assault on David Baltimore," *The New Yorker* (May 27, 1996): 94–109, quote on 102.

Chapter Seven

Giving Back

Time past and time future
What might have been and what has been
Point to one end, which is always present.

—T. S. Eliot

Finding out, figuring out, knowing about the past is only half the job. For me, communicating in some form what I have learned is the reason to engage in local history research in the first place. This may make my local history efforts appear to be utilitarian in the eyes of some. That is the way I am, and I believe that is the way most people are. We learn things about place to understand, to share, to tell others, to explain, and to answer questions that we, and others, have. Anything else, to my mind, would be a one-way conversation.

Knowing leads me to want to share, to contribute to our common knowledge, to show or demonstrate or tell—to teach in its many formats. Learning also leads to asking more questions, questions that are only possible because we have learned and thought about the local past in the first place. Knowledge begets questions; but knowledge is not an end in itself.

Many people begin local history research because they have a specific goal in mind. People research the histories of their own houses or of buildings in their community to document their origins or styles—or to get them listed on an architectural register.

Others begin research about family members in order to construct a genealogy. Some people research the history of a town to write its history or of a church to discuss its background. Many people are interested in the growth of a local industry, spurred by a product they have begun to collect: a bottle, a clock, tools, postcards, even cars or railroad trains. What begins with an interest in an object often expands into a search for information about the

company and then about the industry's role in the history of the community.
Some begin with an interest in the item, then in how the industry came into
being, perhaps to explain the coverlets marked with a date and the town
name, or to document how the manufacture of animal traps helped fund a
different way of life. Some begin research with an eye to creating an exhibit,
and in the process they share what they have learned with others. Some
investigate the ways that the town has grown; others seek to document why a
community has developed in a particular way or what a place used to be like.
Some people engage in local history research in order to assess environmental concerns. The need to know or to understand propels most of us into local
history research. We question, we have been asked to find out, we are curious—and we end up in the local archives.

Beginning with a goal means that we often tailor our research to that end.
When I need to write an article for the newspaper, I research a topic with that
in mind; when I need to give a talk, I search for materials to draw on for that
purpose; when it is time to write a book or create teaching materials, I
approach the archive with readers or students in mind. Thus it is that often we
research with the scope of our research already defined. I do not (usually)
spend fifty hours digging out material for a six-hundred-word article, although I must admit that has happened. In such a small format, I can only use
a bit of information so I try not to go too far beyond what will help me
understand the subject of the article. Of course, I know and need to know
more than I can ever communicate in such a brief space.

Some people speak vaguely about writing a book, as that seems to be an
obvious goal and has been a traditional one. In some cases the book is
actually completed, sometimes it is not. Often a book project hangs like an
albatross around the neck as a constant reminder of work not yet completed.
A book project, however, is not always the ideal format for communicating
local history knowledge, and to simply assume that it is can work to our
disadvantage.

Books, of course, are significant contributions. There are a number of
popular local history book formats. The old eight-hundred-page county history is probably a thing of the past, but smaller, more concise works of local
history will always be popular, as will books of historical photographs, of
now-and-then photographs, of old postcards, and of articles gathered together
around a particular topic. There is a constant need for good well-researched
histories that explain a subject thoroughly. I do not want to imply that a book
is not a proper vehicle for the local historian to consider, because worthwhile
books about local history appear every day. However, we also need articles—scholarly ones for history journals and popular ones such as those
found in airline magazines and tourist brochures and some published by state
or local archives.

Yet not every topic needs to be presented as a book or article, and not every researcher will actually sit down to write, especially when there are so many other interesting formats for local history. The form our research takes will be determined by our own current need, by the nature of the documents we are searching, by our skills, and by the audience we hope to reach.

Exhibits offer a forum for sharing local history research and of late, those I have seen have been very well done. These are usually the creation of historical-society personnel working in local museums and sometimes in other local institutions, especially when an anniversary is about to occur. I would like to see historical exhibits in places other than historical societies. I think we need to have them in banks and on buses, on street bulletin boards, in the county courthouse, and at street festivals and other community events. Only by going outside the historical society will we come into contact with people who have not chosen to expose themselves to local history and who are often surprised by the liveliness of it.

There are many other interesting ways to communicate what we learn, and there are many audiences out there whose interest in local history we should find ways to tap. Because people today have a limited amount of time and many exciting and interesting (electronic) distractions, we need to think of an array of formats in which to display local history. We only get one or, at most, a few opportunities to try to draw people into knowing about the local past. Thus, we must do a good job. And that means knowing what we are talking about and tailoring the form of presentation to the audience and the occasion. The electronic world has made possible individual touring. Many topics fit well into a video presentation, radio presentations, or newspaper discussions, whereas other topics might best become pamphlets, posters, or dramatic presentations.

Probably the most ubiquitous form of local history, and the one encountered by the greatest number of people, is the history article in the local press. Some years ago I put out a call to people who wrote regularly in newspapers. "How did you start?" I asked. Many replied that they had been invited to write by an editor because they were known to have an interest and some knowledge of the subject; some were already on the newspaper staff and took on the job of presenting local history. One man reported that he had bought the newspaper and therefore could put into it what he wanted, so local history was prominently featured.

There are real attractions to writing for the press. Most writers liked the short length of newspaper articles, which run generally from 400 to 750 words for a weekly offering. (Special articles such as anniversary or commemorative pieces, and sometimes obituaries, which are an interesting category of local history unto themselves, are often given somewhat more space.) Some people liked the fact that newspapers often publish pictures, which help explain the topic and often attract readers. For me one of the nicest benefits of writing a newspaper column is that I frequently run into my readers and we can talk. One regular reader is the young man who changes the oil in my car; another is the man who runs the stone quarry.

Writing local history for newspapers requires that the historian view material in small bits. The writing needs to be lively and to the point, and footnotes need to be of the "sneaky" variety (see page 110). Topics usually range over the history of the area, not only in time but in subject and kind, therefore newspaper writing tends to fragment one's attention. A good thing for folks who like to range about, not so good for someone interested in creating more-sustained works.

The conditions of newspaper articles involve questions about using names and events of recent vintage that might upset some readers; pleasing editors while at the same time being true to the standards of historical inquiry; fitting into limited space, which is often inadequate to explain many topics fully; and breaking topics into weekly segments, which might not be totally satisfying. There is also the reality that even if one receives payment, it never begins to cover the costs in terms of the writer's time.

There are joys, however, because a weekly column can be a potent vehicle as the writer gains a degree of local authority, attracting materials that were previously unknown and questions from the public that are sometimes stimulating. A timely column can have an impact on a community, noting an anniversary, a forgotten event, or triggering local memories. When a historic church is threatened by demolition because its congregation wants something modern, an article about the history of the building can make a difference (or exacerbate a split in the church or community). A school board fight might elicit an article about an earlier dispute that could help put the current battle in perspective. A political election might bring forth an article about earlier election shenanigans. A column about diversity at a time of racial or religious tension can help a community see itself in new ways. We should be conscious of the power of the press and the power of the printed word—something that even we local historians can enjoy when writing for hometown newspapers.

What attracted me to writing for the newspaper was that the audience for local history is expanded far beyond those who profess an interest in local history. Even if people are not regular local history readers, a topic one week might pique the interest of some, whereas a different topic another week might attract others. A newspaper allows us to take local history to people other than those who belong to historical societies or attend exhibits and lectures. It offers an expanded and diverse clientele, crossing social, racial, and economic borders, and there are often interesting responses from readers. People call or write to complain, but they also suggest topics and sometimes they share interesting information that might not otherwise be known. Readers have sent me memoirs they have written for senior citizen writing classes, and they have offered up new words, or localisms, or other bits of information that I am happy to receive. Readers, too, alert me to anniversaries, to people, and to events that I might not know about. Readers often remind me that the local historian does not know it all. In general, this is a very satisfactory form of doing local history, and after twenty-five years I have yet to run out of topics. There is always something old to write about.

Shrinking and declining newspapers will diminish space for local history and we who do local history will have to be inventive. I know of local historians who attempt to interest the public via an electronic platform by posting a local picture on the Internet each week with a short commentary, and a number of communities have turned to short radio programs about regional history.

There are other formats to consider. I am a great fan of pamphlets for some of the same reasons that I like writing for the local press. Pamphlets—softcover booklets of up to eighty or so pages—allow us to deal with an event or a trend, to write about a smaller segment of history. The format focuses the topic, which helps the researcher/writer focus the story to be told. There is an economy that I like to be found in pamphlets. Few in the general public these days will sit down to read a four-hundred-page local history—they are generally regarded and used as books of reference. People today are busy and have many choices about what they will read or what they will do. We are competing in a busy market.

Pamphlets are friendly little things. To my mind, they invite people to pick them up and actually read them. Promised within is not an endless discussion or geologic origins, first industries, and early settlers, but a focused one that might be about railroad history, the suffrage movement, or memoirs of World War II, African American life, the development of municipal services—and usually the text is accompanied by pictures. I have a series of pamphlets I have picked up around the country, and I always appreciate the crispness of the presentation, the low cost, and the high quality.

Another form of publication is the four- to eight-page article printed as a separate offering. My model for these is the series of articles about St. Louis neighborhoods published by the Missouri Historical Society that discuss ethnic groups, municipal services, and other topics. These 8 ½ x 11 essays appear in a comfortable format, are illustrated with crisp pictures of the city, and are printed on substantial paper. They are inexpensive to produce and cheap to acquire. The information all these little brochures contain could have been published in book form and it probably would have been bought by the same people who usually purchase historical society materials—and possibly by tourists to St. Louis. Breaking down all this material into discrete segments and publishing them individually makes them attractive to residents and visitors alike. They can be given out by the historical society to visitors, and they can be acquired by teachers to put on classroom walls to show off the city in which their students live.

A number of people have turned to video as a format for presenting local history topics. I have seen some videos that I admire, and I have acted as a consultant in getting one or two of them put together, but I have no expertise about video production or about the costs. Local television stations today often offer classes to teach people how to make videos and then air them on local channels. I have seen some public television programs produced by local people on history topics with variable results—some are well done, others are not quite so smoothly presented. It all depends on the skills of the people involved and probably on the amount of money available to support the project. I would like to see more local historians use this means of communication, perhaps by tapping into the technical resources often available through local community colleges and other local institutions.

Theatrical productions, including dramatic readings, pageants, skits, and choral works, are also potent vehicles for presenting local history. Some years ago, a theater director asked me for the names of interesting local nineteenth-century women she might incorporate into a play. Later, after she had looked at some of the letters and books, she asked me to review her notes, which I did, and in the process I made an arrangement of the materials she had selected and wrote transitions that explained their context.

The script that developed was interesting, but it was only representative of middle-class women. It lacked dimension and breadth, echoing the materials available in the archive but failing to portray a range of nineteenth-century women's lives. When I mentioned this to the director, she asked what documents could be used. I had to explain that there were none—or none I knew of—that illustrated, for example, the lives of Irish serving women or of African American women in our community.

"I could write some material for you," I ventured. I created two characters in the drama that audiences particularly loved. One of the reasons why the fictional characters were especially approachable for both the audience and the actors is that the imagined stories were more completely realized than the snippets that came from letters and diaries of the "real" people. In addition to the fabricated characters—in order to tell the complicated story of one local woman who lived a great long time and vowed at the age of seventeen that she would definitely not want to grow old here—but did!—we put on the stage at the same time her younger and her older self, who was still, at an advanced age, a local resident and a local character.

These were departures from the actual fact, though sound dramatic devices. They made the play popular enough to enjoy several revivals over the past years. But the created characters raise the issue of fictionalizing the past—of mixing the real and the imagined. This can pose difficulties for writer, cast, and audience. The director Oliver Stone has been charged with altering facts in his movies, especially in *JFK* and *Nixon*, and his use of history has been much discussed. Overall, while most people have defended his right to artistic license, many have not approved of altering the well-known and -remembered recent past to create a fabricated story.[1] A stunning recent book that delves into questions about artistic license and the artifice of what historians and historical novelists create is *HHhH* by Laurent Binet (2009). In the process of explaining the murder of Reinhold Heydrich in Prague in 1942, Binet explores questions concerning the writing of history, motivations and actions, and the role of the author—and he is ever present in his book and the reader is grateful to find him there with his witty and wise questions.[2]

We are, however, in a somewhat different relationship to our material than a movie producer or a historical novelist. The local historian or the local historical society has a responsibility to promote a truthful account of the past and is expected to do so. We function, for better or worse, in a climate of few peer reviews and so reviews of our presentations, unlike the multiple protests from many quarters that were raised about Oliver Stone's work.

One of the problems for those charged with or committed to telling the truth about a locality is that the local past is a fragile thing. With relative ease, selected tidbits enter into the public memory, and, right or wrong, they tend to stay there. It is far easier to add a new fact to what the public knows about its local history than it is to erase an error from the local record— especially if the piece of misinformation is an "interesting tidbit." Goodness knows, in my community there are several persistent myths. But, no, the Little Rascals did not originate in Ithaca, the Victorian house on Titus Street was not the model for the Addams Family mansion, and only a few scenes of our gorges and lake appeared in *The Perils of Pauline*. Removing the interesting but incorrect stories about any place is a nightmare.

What, then, is my justification for creating fiction to explain the local past? I see it this way: in many cases there are too few records to represent a particular event and sometimes none for an individual or class of people. In the case of the play about women's lives, there were no documents that allowed us to put on the stage "in their own words" anyone other than white, literate women. To have gone forward with the play without an array of local women would have perpetuated a past we all hope to expand on and not enshrine.

So Elizabeth Blackman in *Between the Lines* tells the audience about her husband, the minister of St. James A.M.E. Zion Church, and about her elder son's occupation as a waiter at the local hotel, and of the blindness of her younger child. Her name and family situation came from the census: her dramatic voice was imagined. Brigid Cain recalls her voyage from Ireland, the opportunities she found in the New World, visits to Ithaca by a priest stationed elsewhere, and the dearth of young Irishmen with the means to marry. In this case too, Brigid's name and status came from the census. These women were real people; their words, however, are imagined, made up, but as true to those women's historical situations as I could imagine them.

These two stories did not expand the local female population to all who might have been included, but they varied the participants in a way that made the play richer and more historically accurate. This is the same justification used for the costumed performers at outdoor museums, those workingmen and -women at the hearth, and even those in the slave auction held at Williamsburg. All of these events are drawn from the historical past and brought to life with words that cannot be quoted from the sources. After years of researching, learning, and reading, there are some things that a historian knows about a place that are not documented and cannot be verified but are useful in creating understanding between then and now, between them and us.

The other reason to turn to fiction in the presentation of the local past has to do with audience. Drama, in particular, offers history in a different venue and sometimes to a broader audience than one finds in a museum setting or reading the local newspaper. Drama and other imaginative forms that use the local past are often useful ways of exploring difficult topics, especially those about which the public might have definite ideas that one would like to question or even dislodge. Where I live, in upstate New York, one of the most problematic topics concerns the Underground Railroad. Many people cling tenaciously to the idea of the railroad, claiming hidey-holes in their homes where there are root cellars, believing in an elaborate pathway north, as clear as a AAA map. Yet the sources are few, and truth hard to ascertain.[3]

To deal with this, I put Harriet Tubman onstage with a speech she never gave. Harriet says, in response to a question about the Underground Railroad:

> Ain't no cars, no tickets, no rails. Mostly it's cellar holes and barn lofts; it is wagons with double floors to hide in, clothes to disguise you, and trunks large enough to fit a man. The Underground Railroad is hiding places and courageous people. People willing to lie to save you even when they hate telling falsehoods. It is those with nerve to do right; to shelter the runaway and risk their freedom to do so. People who pass you on to whoever next is safe. . . . Whoever can be trusted at that moment. Sometime you go one way, sometimes another. It is not a railroad at all, but it is the route to freedom.[4]

This is not the common perception of the Underground Railroad, which by its very name has become in people's minds, and in some artists' renditions, a set route to be followed along populated by people of goodwill. It was much more complicated than that, for sure.

A local theater company has toured two of my historical dramas written for children, this one about the Underground Railroad and another, called *The Day the Women Met*, about the 1848 women's rights convention in Seneca Falls. Each presentation was seen by over fifteen thousand school-children. And each presentation was followed by a question-and-answer session during which the students had a chance to ask the actors questions about the play, about the historical background, and even about the actors themselves.

We knew that the plays worked, for when Harriet Tubman appeared from the bushes carrying her gun, every head in every single audience swung in unison to the left. When Frederick Douglass gave his speech at the 1848 convention there was absolute silence. We knew that the students were engaged. A number of parents who attended the productions made it a point to talk about what the dramatic presentations meant to them. Especially important to many was the presence of minority actors, which noticeably expanded the audience for history.

Whether either of the plays is a good history lesson is harder to assess. The teachers were given packets with information about the plays and about the historical characters, and suggested activities to use in the classroom before the students came to see the presentations. I would assume that the students who were well prepared probably "got more" from the dramatic productions, but we do not know how much of the preshow material was actually used. We do have a huge stack of letters of appreciation from the children, but they were most likely required exercises assigned by the teachers, though some of the kids were genuinely touched by the situations they witnessed. Drama offers a way to show historical events and people and to make actions and dilemmas real and potent. Local history must use every opportunity to present the past in a way that reflects the complexity of life itself. Sometimes fiction provides an important means of presenting the truth about the past.

In fact, historians tend to have two basic responses to historical fiction. One group utterly disdains it. The other group embraces it as interesting, as an alternative way of expanding the audience for history, as a means of telling historical truths that cannot necessarily be documented in the sources, and as genuinely entertaining.

There have been times when historical fiction was our most popular literary form. George Dekker notes that over time "nothing has sold as well as historical fiction." Dekker points to Sir Walter Scott and his Waverley books (circa 1814) as the origin of the historical romance, in which the novel develops a historical consciousness by "multiplying the variety of natural and social forces that impinged on its characters' behavior."[5]

Ernest E. Leisy, who studied and categorized historical fiction, claims there have been three periods when Americans have turned to this genre. The first was the era following 1813 when the nation was creating its own identity. *The Spy* appeared in 1821. James Fenimore Cooper followed the pattern established by Scott in his portrayal of a family divided by partisan interests during the American revolutionary war. This first phase ended with the publication of *Uncle Tom's Cabin*, whose great influence has been acknowledged by many, including Abraham Lincoln, who is said to have referred to its author, Harriet Beecher Stowe, as the "little woman who started the war."[6]

The second period of interest in historical fiction, according to Leisy, was at the turn of the twentieth century. This era also saw the appearance of local color and regional novels, both of which depended on the development of place as well as event. Leisy identifies the third phase of interest in the historical novel as the decades between the 1930s and 1950s. The star attraction during that era was certainly *Gone with the Wind*, which Dekker cites as the most famous and bestselling twentieth-century American historical romance; Wharton's *The Age of Innocence* and Faulkner's *Absalom, Absalom!* were, he claims, "the greatest."[7]

Leisy defends historical fiction as more than escapist literature because it satisfied many tastes, and it satisfied the need of the human mind for a story. He sees it as full of suspense and drama, allowing us to read about people more fully developed than those in traditional books of history. Leisy believes that historical fiction attracts the reader with its "color, pageantry, and the love of excitement."

What is true is that historical fiction has attracted writers of varying abilities and the stories are usually vivid and full of authentic detail. That detail, of course, is what tends to make historical fiction seem so truthful to its readers. Consider the reviews of *Cold Mountain* that commented on Charles Frasier's precise and often arcane vocabulary.[8] Historical fiction has also taken a prominent place in our schools. In preference to using books of history, some elementary-school teachers, I have found, use historical fiction as the basis of their lessons. I talked recently with a fourth-grade teacher who said her entire lesson on abolition and the Underground Railroad came from fictional accounts. This could be seen as a good thing because these books are full of small and telling details and are usually well plotted; it could also be seen as a failure on the part of historians to produce the sort of books that are useful to classroom teachers.

Historical fiction can enlarge the audience for history. The best historical fiction is well written, full of interesting details and stories, and peopled with engaging personalities. These are characteristics that need not be limited to fiction, however, for books of history can also be well written, full of engaging details and interesting characters, and they can surely portray the drama of the past. These are things we local historians need to remember when we sit down to write.

Local historians do a great deal for our communities in terms of answering questions, making people aware of the special places in which we live, and keeping the past alive and relevant to everyday lives. We communicate history in many ways. In return, we also receive a great deal. One of the most satisfying activities that aids me in understanding my hometown, and in knowing how I can talk about it with others, is looking carefully at the place where I live.

In good weather, I perambulate my historical kingdom, if you will, and so should we all. I walk the streets looking at the domestic architecture, the plantings in back and side yards, the evidence of renewal, the loss of community services such as small groceries and repair shops, and the uprisings or the "down-goings" of an area. I think it is important to know my place on foot, rather than through a car window passing by at thirty miles or more per hour, racing to get to other chores, and paying little attention to detail. When we drive we use the streets of our home places, but we do not get to know them intimately.

I perambulate, the very word slowing me down, in order to appreciate what is here and what was there. I look at the evidence of the past that can be seen and note where the street or neighborhood is headed. I perambulate to understand the relationship between places in my city, the distances between places of work and workers' houses, between shops and homes, the distance to school and church. I do this to understand what it was like when this was a walking city, when trips were taken in horse-drawn carriages, then streetcars, and then in slow-moving automobiles. It is only then that the many small neighborhoods begin to make sense, when the duplication of services every few blocks takes on meaning, when I can gauge neighborhood shifts as new areas became fashionable and older areas attracted those less affluent.

I perambulate, too, in order to relive the stories of place. Mostly I walk about in order to recall the people of the past. I remember, at the corner of Plain and Cleveland Streets, Zachariah Tyler and his son John, who lived in two small houses, side by side, their homes metaphors for their partnership in life. In peacetime they worked together as whitewashers, but in 1864, father and son enlisted in the Twenty-Sixth US Colored Infantry and went off to war. In 1865 they returned home from Texas where they had been discharged, Zachariah to preach in various A.M.E. Zion churches and John to become the local ice cream man.

On North Tioga Street I recall the day two workers lost control of a set of trolley wheels that went sailing unimpeded along the tracks into town, the workers racing along behind. I wonder what people thought as they saw those wheels spiraling past them. On North Albany Street I think about the hermit who lived for years and years behind one of the humble houses there, rarely coming out but visited regularly by his cousins, who arrived in swell carriages, watched by the neighborhood children, perched in the large silver maple tree. On State Street I think about one of the city's "Grand Dames" who was known in her later years as the "shopping lady." She had vowed as a teenager—though the term was not used then—not to get stuck in our city, but alas, she did, and she ended her days buying items from the downtown stores, which she carefully carted home but never bothered to unwrap.

At the park in the center of the city I recall the various uses to which it has been put: a place to declaim Independence Day. It was a place of concerts and art shows. In the 1830s it was from this park that the Reverend Samuel Parker left on his journey to take the religious pulse of the Pacific Northwest, as did numerous other missionaries after him, including Dr. Marcus and Narcissa Whitman. Late in the nineteenth century it was the public square where emancipation was celebrated; the site where George Johnson—a colored man, he would have been called then—gave an elegant oration naming those in the city who had aided the cause of the fugitive slave and those who had not. In the 1960s, Martin Luther King spoke in the park. It is a well-used community space.

My perambulations allow me to think about streets and what they were named, how they were improved by the municipality, first with gaslights, then electricity. I consider the various laws enacted to clear the streets of animals, and later of snow; how the shade trees were to be protected from the depredations of horses tethered to the lower branches, and finally laws that regulated the speed of wagons and automobiles.

My perambulations allow me to see, by the arrangement of houses on lots, where serious gardens once existed, edged by fruit trees. And by extension, I can recall the work of planting, and weeding, and hoeing and can think of the kitchen work that followed harvest. I can recall property fashions, too, for at one time fences were important to keep roaming pigs and cows—and even geese—out; now few are to be seen. Today, what were once gardens are more often invaded by plastic swimming pools for the children.

Walking about helps me understand the idea of neighborhood, for even in my small city there were defined areas, each with its own designation, its own character, just as the Missouri Historical Society pamphlet series about neighborhoods. These pamphlets help residents today understand where they live, and they allow those of us with knowledge about place to share it in an inexpensive and accessible format with people who might be unlikely to attend historical society lectures or exhibits.

Our older histories sometimes contain important insights about the places where we live—for an understanding of environmental change is not new. In his 1898 history of Dryden, New York, George Goodrich offers some significant commentaries that have long gone unnoticed but which explain the consequences of certain uses of the land. Dryden in Goodrich's time was a prosperous village supporting fifty-three sawmills, all run by waterpower. He noted, however, that deforestation was necessary so that agriculture could flourish and the mills could produce lumber. Later, he observed that the consequence of all this timbering was that residents had more snow to deal with. In the early days the heavy forest protected inhabitants from snow and wind. He insisted snowdrifts were unknown, but with the trees gone, the wind cut across open fields and piled snow as high as a man could stand. Finally, Goodrich suggested that malignant typhoid fever developed throughout the area because the lowlands had been deprived of their natural foliage and the town had not yet established artificial or effective means of drainage.

Knowledge of place, an understanding of where we live, can bring pleasure to those who live there. But it is also a crucial factor in our sense of responsibility to the land, for to understand the past of an area is to also foster its care.

We have returned to a consideration of the land where we live, much as William Lambarde did in 1576, when he wrote his book *The Perambulation of Kent*, and as George Goodrich did in explaining the changes in Dryden. Our hikes across the terrain of our home place link us to the land, as does our current historical interest in public space, the development of civic responsibility, architectural change, the market economy, and so much more. We perambulate in order to understand, to sense how a place was used in other times, and to see the consequences of that use so that we can communicate the complexity of the palimpsest on which we live to those who depend on us for understanding.

NOTES

1. For essays about how Hollywood has used history, see Marc A. Carnes, ed., *Past Imperfect: History According to the Movies* (New York: H. Holt, 1995). There are a number of other books that deal with this issue. Two books by Robert Brent Toplin are important: *History by Hollywood: The Use and Abuse of the American Past* (Urbana: University of Illinois Press, 1996) and Oliver Stone's *USA: Film, History, and Controversy* (Lawrence: University of Kansas Press, 2000).

2. Laurent Binet, *HHhH* (Paris: Grasset and Fasquelle, 2009).

3. See Milton C. Sernett, *North Star Country: Upstate New York and the Crusade for African American Freedom* (Syracuse: Syracuse University Press, 2002).

4. From *Escape to the North*, presented by the Center for the Arts in Ithaca, during winter 1999 as part of the Hangar Theater's Educational Outreach program run by Lisa Bushlow, director of the Center for the Arts in Ithaca. In 2001, this program presented *The Day the Women Met*.

5. George Dekker, *The American Historical Romance* (New York: Cambridge University Press, 1987).

6. Robert A. Lively, *Fiction Fights the Civil War* (Chapel Hill: University of North Carolina Press, 1957).

7. Ernest E. Leisy, *The American Historical Novel* (Norman: University of Oklahoma Press, 1950).

8. Charles Frasier, *Cold Mountain* (New York: Atlantic Monthly Press, 1997).

Coda to Chapter 7

The Great Document Exchange

It has long interested me that in order to read about the early days in the Oregon Territory we need to go to New York State, where Narcissa Whitman's letters were sent. To know about English and Irish emigrants to the United States and the lives they led in our communities, we need to search archives in Great Britain. To know what soldiers felt, how they reacted to the terrain, and what they saw when they went off to the Mexican War, we look not at battlefield sites but in the records in their various hometowns. So, too, we learn about the California gold rush by looking in New England, Pennsylvania, and Virginia for letters in archives and those published in local newspapers from Argonauts describing their crossing of Kansas, the intermountain West, or the Southwest. We find out about conditions in Florida during World War II by reading letters written home by soldiers stationed there: soldiers who, living elsewhere in civilian life, found Florida "something to write home about."

None of this is surprising. A letter from one person to another in the same town is rarely descriptive of place; both, after all, live in the community and presumably know what the area looks like, what is going on. This is not to say that local letters are not important; but it is to suggest that people look more closely at the local terrain and situation when they try to tell others what a place is like. Diary keepers are generally more descriptive of place when they go elsewhere and create travel journals. The point of this is that in all our archives and repositories, even in the letters still in attics and garages, there is a great deal of information about "other places." That is, the place from which the letter was written, where the diary was created, or where the writer was at the time of writing.

Elizabeth Fuller, the librarian at the Westchester County Historical Society, a county two hundred miles distant from my home, sent me a letter that had originated in my county in 1823. She asked me to write a comment about it for her society's historical journal, which I was really happy to do.

What a delight! Here was a letter I knew nothing about, describing Enfield, a part of my county for which there is relatively little—well, truthfully, hardly any—descriptive material, at a time when the area was first being settled. Here was information about people who first farmed the area, about their doings, their origins. This is material that is very important for my community's historical record, but it resides in another place altogether. I knew nothing about this letter, and I suspect that other historians in my county do not either.

Suddenly, I had this wondrous vision. I imagined that one calm, sunny day, from all over the country, letters, diary entries, journals, and newspaper accounts would all rise gently from the communities where they reside, to hover and then flutter in the sky above. In my vision, the sky became full, and there were white envelopes everywhere, wafting calmly above the treetops. Then, softly, all these floating documents descended to earth, heading homeward. (That I live in a community with a great deal of snow, and that this thought occurred in the winter, might have something to do with this miraculous epiphany!)

From that vision of rising documents, I conjured up the idea of a Great Letter Exchange. On some designated day, archivists and local historians everywhere in the country would draw from their local collections a single letter that describes another place. It could be a letter from San Diego when that place was a distant community struggling to survive, a newspaper account written by a visitor to an agricultural fair in Nashville, a letter telling about an execution held behind the town jail viewed by a traveler passing through Tucson, a journal entry describing Altoona by a traveler on the railroad, or a description of the irritation felt by the missionaries in Hawaii concerning the mores of the businessmen living there.

With the aid of a copy machine, the document would be duplicated, placed in an envelope, and sent to the keeper of that other community's history. Everyone in a careful, yet random fashion would give something, contribute something, to another community's knowledge of its past.

And just as casually, a day or two or several days later, the envelopes would arrive. An offering from Scarsdale might descend on Phoenix; an envelope from Norfolk would arrive in Independence; something from Portland, Oregon, might go to Portland, Maine; from Andover, Massachusetts, to Austin; from Chicago to Key West. From those envelopes, archivists and local historians everywhere would pull documents describing their own place—events and times of long ago, and not so long ago, with which they become richer. And in making this curious journey home, the document adds to the descriptions and knowledge of our communities and illustrates the links between us.

Can you imagine the pleasure of opening such a letter? Suddenly in your hands is a new description of your home place, a fresh view of something known or something new, an additional piece of the historical picture of the past that we are all, always, trying to add to—absolute completion being beyond any possibility. We would see our own history grow fuller, while, in addition, we would have evidence of a crucial lesson for our friends and neighbors. This Great Document Exchange would demonstrate the importance of personal observation, of writing, and of saving source materials. It would reiterate the lesson so many of us try to teach: that each and every one of us is an actor in history, a participant in times that will soon become The Past, and that we are all capable of adding to the historical record.

In today's world this great document exchange could happen even more easily via the Internet—and the connection of one place to another could occur at the touch of the send button: not as heady a vision as envelopes snowing down on us, but equally helpful.

Recently I saw a bumper sticker on a car that commanded me to "Commit Random Acts of Kindness." What a lovely thought. Perhaps the cars of archivists, preservationists, and local historians should carry a similar sign: Commit Random Acts of Archival Exchange. And who better than the American Association for State and Local History to promote this wonderful event?

The Great Document Exchange could become an annual event, and we might celebrate Document Exchange Day—perhaps during Archives Week. What a grand way to create national publicity and interest in local history. Now, wouldn't that be something?

Chapter Eight

The Local Historian

I summon to my aid the muse of local History—the traditions of our own home—the chronicles of our own section—the deeds of our native heroes.
  —William Gilmore Simms, *Katharine Walton: or, The Rebel of Dorchester* (1851)[1]

A local historian must be and do many things. If I were to advertise for a person to fill the position, I would mention some obvious skills and some that are not so obvious. A local historian must be a multifaceted individual—with a good deal of stamina—a person who is self-motivated and happy to work alone, yet someone who works well cooperatively too, a person who cares to get the whole story and to get it as accurately as possible.

The obvious: Local historians first and foremost engage in research. They may specialize in land transactions of early settlers, in the impact of technology on their towns, or on industries and products, but they are generally expected to know something about just about everything. Even then, a specific question can easily raise a topic about which the local historian knows nothing, for no one can know it all. Admitting that, to others and one's self, often helps.

Local history research leads in many directions. Just as often as there is success, there is the hollow, knowing feeling that a search has run its course, that the materials are just not there to be found. In success or frustration, in traditional source materials or in items we are just learning to use and appreciate, many local historians regard research as the best part of the job.

Local historians also collect and preserve materials. In places where there are officially appointed historians (most specifically Indiana and New York), this is often the most important official function they perform.[2] Seeking out new material and preserving older documents are important activities. Local historians are also frequently asked for advice concerning materials that indi-

viduals and institutions need to preserve or interpret. They, well, we, answer
questions about environmental concerns, historic structures, and the natural
history of streams and rivers in a community.

Local historians communicate their interests and concerns in a number of
ways, apprising the public of upcoming anniversaries, alerting people to the
possible destruction of structures of historical significance, teaching about
the value of documents, and answering questions. These questions come in
great numbers, even more now than previously because so many arrive via
the Internet. Most of those are genealogical concerns; many are from the
media; some are from preservationists; others come from researchers seeking
documents; and any number of questions are asked by schoolchildren.

It is not so obvious, but local historians, who are usually defined by
geographical location, need to know that history bleeds across borders and
that there is much to learn even outside a designated place: people, after all,
lived their lives without regard to town or county lines, so materials about
one place are likely to be found in the archive there and in repositories
nearby. Local historians need to read not only about their community's history but also about history in general, about other communities, and about
topics. This broader reading not only informs but can suggest questions and
can introduce topics that might not otherwise be thought of.

Theodore Zeldin, the historian of France, has noted that historians need
"imagination" and that imagination is "as important to historians as new
documents."[3] Professor Zeldin is not suggesting that we make up history but,
rather, that we approach the documents of local history with the imagination
to understand viewpoints of the past, to picture the landscape, and to breathe
life into the documents we have. I am often struck by the usefulness of place
to writers of detective fiction. Place becomes a character and use of place,
either an imaginary one such as St. Mary Wood in Agatha Christie's books,
or Paris in the stories of Georges Simenon, plays a decided role. That ability
to write about the landscape and to make the reader feel it is something that
an imaginative local historian might consider. Our plots do not involve murder, most usually, nor do most of us make the settings of our histories as
vivid as those who have a crime to solve.

It is obvious also that fairness and open-mindedness are important for a
local historian. We cannot suppress material because we do not like it. We
cannot ignore material because it does not fit set ideas—ours or anyone
else's. We cannot be blind to contradictions that emerge. Often the written
documents fail to substantiate an oral tradition—and such a discrepancy
cannot be overlooked. Instead, inconsistencies need to be explored—and the
long-accepted, but untrue, version should be explained. Getting it out of the
public memory is another thing altogether, but ours is the job of getting
things straight—or as straight as possible. It is the local historian who can
demonstrate to the community not only what the records reveal (the truth)

but why another, even a popular version (the local myth) took hold and then held on, which means that the local historian deals with the past and also the memory of the past: that is not always such an obvious task, but it is an important one.

A local historian should see particularity and specificity in the past, but these should be placed in the appropriate context. Thus, a local historian turns a microscope on a geographic area to understand how events known to be happening elsewhere were played out on this smaller stage. Thus we look for the effects of the Civil War even in places where battles did not occur, or how a destructive storm affected a region, not only one place. The good local historian uses a telescope too; to balance the delight of knowing particular things about a locality, a longer, larger lens affords a broad knowledge of regional and national history, so that events of one's town are placed in perspective. Not every local event is unique—but some are. It takes a knowledgeable historian to distinguish between the two and to know when to describe a general pattern and when to claim something truly unusual. This balance is a crucial aspect of what the local historian must do. It is a task that calls for a microscope to see particular events and a telescope to see general patterns. So my want ad for a local historian would look something like this:

> WANTED: Local Historian, skilled at reading history, asking questions, using historical imagination; needs knowledge of how to collect and preserve historical materials and how to pursue historical research; strong communication skills.
> Knowledge of community important; open-mindedness, fairness, and perseverance a necessity.

There are occupational hazards that local historians face. A major hazard is that we research and write the histories of the communities in which we live. This can color our perspective. Most academic historians do not remain long in or write extensively or exclusively about one community. If they do write a community history at one time, their next work is apt to be on another subject. Rarely will an academic historian pursue the history of one community throughout an entire career, although the exception that might prove the rule could be Blake McKelvey, who lived in Rochester, New York, for many years and wrote about that city, or Constance McLaughlin Greene, who wrote extensively about Washington, D.C. Academic historians have a broad range from which to draw documentary resources, and most often they do not live among the people about whom they write. This gives them a distance that can be useful, especially when there are events that locals might think are uncomplimentary. Local historians' closeness to place has its dividends and its drawbacks. Among the benefits is the close proximity of sources of information—often information comes knocking in the form of family documents, old photographs, or collections that others have made. Local histo-

rians know the terrain and understand the close meanings of words and
expressions that people in the area use. We also know the probable places to
look for evidence and often the people or the family of people—or neighbors
of those involved. This provides an ease of access often unmatched for academic historians.

This familiarity, however, is sometimes a disadvantage. People in a locality usually expect that their history will be written to a certain standard,
usually promotional, style. Few local historians care to broach topics about
which there is community silence, for were they to do so there could be a loss
of local trust: sources can suddenly dry up and support or documents be
withheld. Consider the plight of Anna Rosmus, the German teenager who
turned a successful history of her hometown of Passau into research that
exposed its secret Nazi past. The 1990 movie *The Nasty Girl* is based on her
research and details her subsequent treatment by her neighbors when they
discovered what she was up to. The townspeople were not interested in
having their remembered past explored and exposed.[4]

Our communities expect local history to be boosterish. Often local historians not only accept this view, but allow it to color the type and range of
topics on which they work. Of course, this is not to say that local historians
are only interested in gossip or dirty linen. As one local historian wrote to
me, most people in a community know the local stories—long before the
local historian goes to work. What they do not approve of, however, is
reviving the story, putting it into print, and making it available to others.
Where is the line between gossip and historical topic? What subjects can and
should be pursued in a local history?

What does a local historian do with dirty linen? In general, the specifics
of a story are probably not of great interest and we are not out to expose a
personal situation. Yet, when research touches on a trend or theme, then that
can be investigated. The uncomfortable bits are part of history too and we
need to find ways of dealing with them. The Ku Klux Klan activity of the
1920s is a subject that makes people profoundly uncomfortable, as does
discussion of the race riots of the 1960s; yet tragedies—natural and those of
human making—most certainly need to be dealt with.

Consider, for example, this situation from my local area. In the 1860s, a
woman poisoned her two teenaged daughters and probably several others as
well. There was a trial, and she was found guilty. She was sent to an asylum
for the insane, where she later died. Do we use the woman's name, especially
considering there is family still in the area? Do we use the name when there
is a local store known by that name? When I was going to write about this
episode in an article about this nineteenth-century woman and crime, I mentioned it to the present owner of the store, who is no relation. He was glad to
know beforehand but had no qualms about the name appearing in the local

press as the incident had happened over one hundred years ago. Still, hearing of this case caused people to think there might be a connection.

What if, on the other hand, a scandal involved some betrayal of the public trust? What if the heir of the town's most respected family caused the family bank to fail? Here the personal act becomes part of a larger picture and one that touches on the loss of the financial institution for the community and the consequences for people whose investments it had held. In this case, the failure of the bank places the family in the middle of the story. "I would not write the story of such a failure," said one local historian to me with a glinting eye, daring me to say that I would. But I think that I might. Here, my editor challenges me: Would I now, as an experienced local historian, write about this episode? Would I have done so when I was just starting out? Well, both, probably. Today I would write the story because I am interested in what happens to people when their savings are gone, when they need to start over, especially when it happened at a time when there was little public assistance available. To whom did those who lost their savings turn? How did they cope? Did they remain in the community, or did they leave? When I was younger I would still have been interested in these same questions, and I think I would have written the same story. A bank failure is an important event. It affects the community, and it affects individuals. From such an investigation we can learn a good deal.

Peggy Korsmo-Kennon, director of the Waseca County (Wisconsin) Historical Society at the time when I met her some years ago, sent me an interesting problem concerning an individual's right to privacy. In a community history published in 1980, there is mention of a 1952 murder. Writing some thirty years after the event, the author notes that "few criminal trials have aroused greater interest," in the town. Included in the history are three paragraphs about the murder and the punishment meted out. There is also an excerpt from the trial proceedings that had appeared in the newspaper. A problem arose, however, because the man convicted of the murder—an instance of domestic violence in which a police officer was killed—had served his time in jail and was, at the time of the publication of the local history, free and living nearby. When he read about himself in the history he promptly sued the sponsor of the book and the historian on the grounds that he had paid for his crime and therefore should not be tarred further by it. It is a murky area of the law, but, according to my very generalized knowledge of the law, it is difficult for someone to win this kind of privacy suit unless the person can also show that some of the published information is false. Still, the instance is a caution; what we write carries a local impact, sometimes far beyond what we can envision.

The answer to the problem of a subject's privacy must be found by each historian in how the material in question is to be used and for what purpose. And there are always new twists on this problem. Helen Hooven Santmyer, author of *Ohio Town: A Portrait of Xenia*, an admirable history, discusses information that came to her along with an 1886 and 1887 survey conducted by the Board of Health in which each home in the community was examined and its condition noted. Santmyer decided, "As for its scatological aspect— that in itself is material for pages of comment. It is a disillusioning subject, however, and best let alone." Too bad. That sort of information could prove to be tremendously revealing.[5] The local historian might use the data as the basis of a discussion of the health problems identified in the community at that time, of common home situations deemed worthy of public concern, of education levels, and of race, ethnicity, and class. How were the problems addressed? What public measures were taken? Were there follow-up studies? We should fall happily on such material as a great bonus to what we know about times past.

Another common condition of doing local history is that most local historians work alone. There are usually but one or two historians in a community, and there is not always an easy communication between them. Nor do local historians, in general, talk with, compare notes with, discuss problems with, or debate issues with historians in other communities. All aspects of our work suffer because of this: we do not get the aid of others who might know something about the topic on which we are laboring; we do not get to make comparisons with other places; we usually do not have the benefit of someone else reading our material before it goes to press. We fail to have a sense of knowing that other people are thinking about the same issues we are or are even interested in the questions we ask.

In many ways, this isolation is lessening, as there are more and more opportunities for regional historical organizations, academic conferences, and now the Internet with its great sense of collectivity, all that pull historians together to talk to each other. But this is not always the case. There are some obvious ways of correcting this situation. The American Association for State and Local History (AASLH) provides a newsletter and a quarterly magazine, *History News*. There are regional and statewide annual conventions that can provide community and information. The National Council on Public History publishes the journal *The Public Historian*, which includes reviews of books on local history in addition to helpful reviews of historical exhibits and films.[6] In addition, state historical societies are sometimes effective in setting up seminars and workshops for local historians. It is smart to join whatever groups gather nearby local historians together in informal settings to discuss announced topics. (Do see the coda to this chapter.) A great source of historical companionship and help is available on the Internet. Begin with H-Local at http://www.h-net.msn/~local and see what your state has to offer.

There is also the edgy issue of what a community thinks of its local history, of those who "do" it, and how they should be compensated. In many places members of the community regard the local historian as a public resource. I believe the reasoning goes something like this: what that person does is my history, the history of my community; therefore that person should give me any help I need—which frequently means that the local historian is asked to speak and contribute without anyone seeing the need to provide payment for that labor.

We do not, however, make speeches without a great deal of preparation; we do not write articles without research and then whatever degree of struggle there might be to write, edit, refine, and make it the best we can. Were the school district to ask a psychologist to give a talk, there would be no hesitation in providing payment. When it is the local historian who is asked to take over a class, however, school officials are often surprised that payment might be appropriate and expected. I suspect that we are partially at fault for being so free with our time and knowledge because we want to be helpful and to get the history straight. We might need to set a higher value on what we do, so that other people will value it as we do yet there is a tradition of being regarded as a community resource—a role we want to play while the work behind the expertise (lecture, article, book) is taken for granted.

This is not, however, a simple issue; nor is it one for which I necessarily have useful answers. If you are a local historian, value yourself and your work. Investigate what other self-employed people charge for their time and what they donate to their communities. Talk with local historians in other communities (if only on the Internet) about what they do or wish they had done. Be clear with yourself ahead of time so that you can be forthright with those who ask for your help. Be prepared to say: "I normally charge $X/hour for that type of work. Would you like me to provide a quote?" or "I normally cannot provide such services for free, but I'd be happy to make a donation in this case." It is best to be prepared by thinking about the issue beforehand so that you have some responses to fit situations you can reasonably expect to encounter. If we value our work as professionals and communicate that to our potential audiences, then we have a better hope of changing old patterns. A note: I come from a generation of volunteers. Young people today are more forthright about seeing monetary value in what they do and expecting compensation for work accomplished. This might be my problem more than yours.

The public schools pose obvious opportunities and some complexities. I am often amazed at how effectively any number of teachers manage and what a lasting impact lessons in local history often have on students. We are all happy to see youngsters engaged in asking questions about the places in which they live, and those questions are often valuable teaching moments. How do we know that, a student will ask? How can we find out, the good teacher muses?

Local history courses in the public schools occurred in the twentieth century. For example, the North Carolina Literary and Historical Association began assisting the public schools teach local history by distributing pamphlets on assorted subjects, and then in 1907 the state legislature charged the North Carolina Historical Commission to "encourage the study of North Carolina history in the schools of the state." Other states date the teaching of local history to those early days. New York began its program in local history in the early 1940s as a way of introducing patriotism. Yet any number of states mandated local history instruction in the 1980s and 1990s (Georgia, Delaware, Arkansas, Nebraska) and Colorado did so in 2009. At the same time, states, faced with new challenges, were also eliminating local history courses and by the end of the twentieth century, courses in state history presented on the campuses of state universities were abandoned.

In only a few instances were the teachers in the fourth and seventh grades prepared to teach local history: few had had a course in state history, few knew anything historical methods, and most who offered it taught themselves—and did so admirably. They drew on local sources, including local historians, and in some cases made lasting impressions on their students. This is the obvious opportunity for interest in local history.

Class assignments were often imaginative. National History Day (NHD), begun in 1974, attracted a good deal of attention and used history to challenge students to engage in research projects. By 1980, nineteen states participated with funding from the National Endowment for the Humanities expanding over the next decade and in 2012 NHD received the National Humanities Medal from President Barack Obama, so effective had the program become.

The problem often, however, was that what seemed to be a good topic to research could not be well supported by local resources, being too broad—or too narrow—and topics were often misinterpreted by students.

One Monday I had a phone call from a ninth grader named Gordon. "Could you help me?" he asked. He explained: "I am writing a paper for my teacher on Ithaca's history. Could we meet to talk about it?"

My antenna went up. "What is the topic of your paper?" I asked.

"Settlement," he said. "I want to write about who came and why. I have been reading about the Sullivan Campaign. . . ."

"Those are two different subjects," I interjected. "Related, for sure, in some cases, but two different topics. How long is your paper supposed to be?"

About four pages, he guessed, but he did not seem sure. "Well, then, we need to get a focus. What do you really want to write about? There is Sullivan's Campaign and there is the settlement era. Do you know when settlement began?"

"Well, no," he said.

"What have you read?" He named the standard nineteenth-century county history that runs over a thousand pages. He certainly had not read all of that: no one has!

"The 1894 book?"

"That one," he said.

"And what did you learn?"

"That Sullivan's Campaign is interesting."

"Indeed it is. But it really isn't about settlement, at least not directly. When did the military campaign take place?" I asked in my most teacherly voice. There was silence. I answered for him. "In 1779. When did the revolutionary war end?" I asked again.

"1776?"

"1783. But settlement in this part of the state only began in the early 1790s."

"Oh," he said.

"So pick one: Sullivan or settlement. You only have four pages, remember."

"Well, I am interested in the settlement era, why people came out here."

"Okay. That's good. Now what do you know about that?"

"Well," he began, and then there was silence.

"Okay. Let's focus on who came and why. Does that interest you?"

"Yes."

"Do you know anything about the Military Tract?"

"I have heard of it . . . I think."

"Okay. The Military Tract was land given to veterans of the revolutionary war as payment for their service. The state didn't have any money to pay the soldiers, so many of them fought for the promise of getting land afterward."

"So they came out here?"

"Well, not so fast. Some did. Some didn't. In fact, probably most of those who got land didn't. So we have to figure out why."

"Why?"

"Well, you and I can figure that out after you read a little about the period and you write down what the topic is that you are interested in—just on a slip of paper, so you and I know exactly what you are going to do. By the way, how soon does this paper have to be handed in?"

"Pretty soon, I guess. Friday?"

"Okay. We'd better get to work."

Now I know that you are not interested in the local history of my place, but this scenario can be heard from Alaska to Florida, with the events changed but the players the same. And this episode involves some real problems that local historians and teachers have to face.

The first concerns the assignments that teachers give to students, for they are not always clearly stated. Teachers often let students go off thinking that in four pages (double spaced) they can write the history of an entire town. The second problem concerns students' understanding of the assignment. We all know that no matter how well focused, clearly explained, and logical an assignment might be, students often go away not getting what it is they are supposed to do. Librarians face this problem all the time—even in prestigious university libraries.

The third problem is that doing local history research is not easy; the materials are not always there; all questions cannot be answered; some questions are more complex than they appear to be on the surface; and students, especially those in the fourth and seventh grades, when local history is most often assigned, are not prepared for the use of original documents, the lack of information, and the conflicting nature of the material.

There is the additional problem of sending young students to very outmoded books when there are better texts available—often right there in the school library—but sometimes the teachers do not know the subject well enough to know what the best resources for local history are. Suggesting that students call the local expert is an easy way out. This raises the problem of sending students off to find the local expert, which in this case turned out to be me. I am happy to help, we are all happy to help, but without knowing anything about the assignment we are apt to lead students to more material than they really need to look at or to more complex renderings of the material when they were directed to the topic for some other pedagogical reason having little to do with the topic at hand.

This problem is even more complex because if even one student, not to mention six or seven, gets a local historian or local historical society archivist on the phone, this can be very time-consuming. There is an assumption that I should spend any number of hours with students figuring out what the assignment is, what the topic of interest is, and all the other processes that go into leading someone into local history research.

Sure, our job is to help others learn local history, and it is the aspect of being a local historian that I like best. But the annual inundation of questions from students can be wearying, especially when we have other work on our desks. Students should come to us. But they should come well prepared so that we do not have to do the work that they and their teachers should have done to begin with. I like to explain to students and others how to find the information needed, where to look, even what books or papers to trust. I don't much like doing their work for them.

One solution is for teachers to consult with local history experts before handing out assignments. They might request a list of topics and sources that can be researched with some ease by students in their grade. Another solution is for teachers to experience local history research themselves so that they understand the process. This happens far too infrequently, and in a way it is our own fault because local historians often hand out information without involving questioners themselves in the process of doing history. The bottom line is that teachers need to understand historical research, and local historians and historical societies need to be regarded as history consultants and not as encyclopedias. This is perhaps the easy answer to a complex question. At the very least, everyone concerned would benefit from improved communication.

The ideal solution would be for school districts to hire local historians to give local history seminars for teachers interested in using local history in the classroom. Were the matter at hand the use of computers, or new math, or reading strategies, school districts would have experts to teach the teachers before they needed to broach the subject in the classroom. The same should be true of local history, for as simple as it seems from the outside, we all know that local history research, while fun and rewarding, can be a can of local worms!

My interest in all this is to get the student, of whatever age, to a manageable topic that is possible to do successfully. This is no less a goal than the teacher has!

Local historians do obvious things for a community. But there are also tasks that are not straightforward. What we learn when we research a topic is often only understood because it comes on top of, or after, other history learned. A local historian is someone, at the end, who is careful and engaged.

NOTES

1. *Katharine Walton: or, The Rebel of Dorchester* (New York: Redfield, 1853), 2.
2. See David G. Vanderstel, "County Historians," in *Encyclopedia of Local History*, ed. Carol Kammen and Amy H. Wilson (AltaMira Press, 2012), 114–19.
3. Theodore Zeldin, "Personal History and the History of the Emotions," *Journal of Social History* 15 (Spring 1982): 341–42.
4. *The Nasty Girl* is part of a trilogy. The other movies are *The White Rose* (1982) and *My Mother's Courage* (1995), directed by Michael Verhoeven. *The Nasty Girl* won several awards, including the Silver Ear Award at the Berlin Film Festival.
5. Helen Hooven Santmyer, *Ohio Town: A Portrait of Xenia* (New York: Harper and Row, 1984), 90.
6. *The Public Historian* has been edited at the University of California at Santa Barbara since 1978. It contains articles and reviews of recent books, films, and museum exhibits, and often there are essay debates that present a variety of views. See, in particular, the roundtable devoted to the subject of public history and memory, particularly Michael Frisch, "What Public History Offers, and Why It Matters," *The Public Historian* (Spring 1997): 31–40. The address of this journal is in care of the editor, Department of History, University of California, Santa Barbara, CA 93106-9410. See also Alan S. Newell, "Public History," in *Encyclopedia of Local History*, 473–76.

Coda to Chapter 8

Adult Local-History Workshops

There are many routes people take to become local historians. Some are born into the position: "Dad was, and now I am." Others find the title thrust upon them: "When Mother died I found people just assumed that I would take over, especially since I inherited her records, so they call me when they have questions."

Others find that curiosity leads them to find out about a facet of the community, and that becomes enough to establish them as "experts" to whom others come for information. Knowing one thing often leads to becoming interested in knowing how to find out other things. Sometimes this path is taken by newcomers seeking information and involvement with a new place—a bare-rooted person taking hold in a place. Genealogical and architectural interests often lead people into deeper local history research.

Some teachers find themselves unprepared but, nonetheless, are asked to teach local history. That experience, with too little information and lacking a prepared curriculum, often leads to a greater involvement with local history. Some people majored in history in college or liked it in high school and find that doing local history is a way of continuing that interest even if their professional lives take other turns. Others disliked high-school history and find to their surprise that settled in a place, history has its charms. Others live near the historical society and are pulled in by programs or interesting exhibits. There are some, of course, who go to school expecting to work in the local or public history field. These are people who learn a wide variety of useful skills and can move from one community to another in order to practice their craft.

Regardless of the roads that people take to become local historians, once established as local authorities, most assume a posture of immortality. That is, many people who have become local historians fail to take into consideration the fact that they will not last forever. So while local historians collect, protect, educate, exhibit, research, and write about the history of place, rarely do they take the time to wonder who will take over when it comes time for them to transfer to the great Archive in the Sky—or wherever it is that local historians go.

Rarely do local historians regard it as their duty to train others to take over the tasks of doing local history. It is easier to assume that other people will find their way into local history in the same haphazard way that they did. And it happens.

But wouldn't it be far better if, instead of relying on chance, we actually thought about preparing for the future while we are still here to comment on that trove of letters in old Mrs. Smith's attic that one needs to keep an eye on, or to advise about the unreliability of the standard late-nineteenth-century history of the town, or to pass on that one crucial fact in order to follow the current thinking about "The Big Local Topic"? In other words, wouldn't it be nice to have a word or two with one's successor?

Wouldn't it be a gift to the person who follows to know that he or she does not need to learn everything all over again, as we had to do, but could come prepared, knowing how to conduct local research, how to ask good questions about a place, how to put the locality in a regional and even a national context? Wouldn't it be a good idea if local historians took on apprentices? Or, barring that, if local historians conducted classes or exercises to teach others skills?

One solution, and it might not be everyone's, is to invite applicants to join an adult local history workshop. These should be limited to a small number of people; there need be no costs; and participation for the duration of a year should be expected. Participants may come from those long rooted in the community or the recently replanted. In either case, it is interest and dedication that are most wanted.

A number of topics might be given to the group to consider, and, within a reasonable amount of time, the group would be asked to decide which one to take on. Some possible topics might include

- the depression of the 1930s
- our county in the Civil War era
- World War II and the locality
- political history
- race and ethnicity
- technology and change
- family life over the past fifty years

• protests/community disputes

These are broad but also clearly defined topics. I would expect the discussion of which topic to select would involve everyone in the group and focus on how one goes about learning something about the locality. This exercise would be an important lesson in itself.

Once a topic has been decided upon, the group should engage in background reading, determine a work plan, and divide the research tasks among individuals or assign them to one or two people who might want to work together. This second phase might take several months as each aspect of the topic is explored. Monthly reports would reveal the aspects of the research that need to be refined and would help keep everyone up to date with all parts of the research. These meetings could also provide minor deadlines so that work progresses steadily.

While the research phase is under way, there should be discussions of what else needs to be explored, where to find additional information, what might be available elsewhere, and how best to communicate the results of the work. It might be that the topic and material should be shared in visual ways, or that something should be written up, or that the subject would work best as an ongoing dialogue that might occur in a number of places such as at a local historical society, in the newspaper, in the schools, or on the local television station. It might also be possible, depending on the skills of the participants, to have a variety of ways of disseminating the information gathered and the conclusions drawn about the topic. Certainly, the electronic media will play a significant role in whatever is unearthed.

Throughout, the goal for the participants would be to work together to understand the topic. But the secondary goal, in my view, is to enhance the research expertise of the group and develop thinking about history. These are valuable tools that will easily carry over into other projects. At some point, it will be easy for the group's leader to step aside, knowing that there is a trained group of people who can comfortably take over the researching and communicating of local history.

This workshop idea is not new. In England there have been a series of Adult Local History Workshops held on a variety of topics aimed at exploring local history and at the same time teaching local history techniques. Do look at *Group Projects in Local History*, edited by Alan Rogers, published in 1977 by Dawson Publishing, Kent, England.

The English have devised some interesting ways of educating people interested in local history. In this country we have thought less about such things. A local history workshop might provide one relatively easy and local means of providing education in a context that is friendly, supportive, and interesting, in addition to being useful for the community.

Chapter Nine

The Past That Was Yesterday

Willing oneself into nostalgia for the present can, at times, make one see the beauty of what is near at hand. The world is still here for us.
—Howard Mansfield, *In the Memory House*[1]

There is little doubt that for the last twenty-five years of the twentieth century, local history was on a roll. It was recognized, funded better than ever before, of interest to a wide range of people, and it was thought to be useful. Local history was written and read; it provided source materials for students, and from local documents scholars have discerned patterns and models. I would date the revival of interest in local history—or perhaps I should say a broadly based concern for it—to the Bicentennial of the American Revolution in 1976: an easy date to focus on.

This was not the situation for local history earlier. Prior to 1976, local historical societies were—in general—doing things as they had always been done: membership was restricted by habit to local elites, to those who found antiquarian pursuits compatible, and to the elderly—or at least those over the age of fifty. Few historical societies did more than collect the artifacts of prominent families, sponsor lectures that were in general poorly attended, and host genealogists who came to use the documents kept in historical society archives. I do realize that there were some exceptions, but, in general, historical societies were rather musty places. They were dependent on a few who, over and over again, elected themselves to the boards of trustees; they reached out almost not at all; and they expected to continue with dim lighting and inadequate captions for objects that were rarely dusted or replaced. They were places visited by schoolchildren, places occupying old houses or rooms somewhere, places that survived on infusions of money from wills and trusts and membership dues of two or five dollars.

Interestingly, a good deal of local history was published in the 1950s. Though shorter in length, most histories tended to mimic those of the nineteenth century. The topics that came under consideration were much the same as those in earlier days. Public talks tended to focus on battles, on Indians, archaeological ruins, or on local industries. The staff was usually comprised of volunteers, and those who were paid were mostly untrained— though many were highly effective in keeping local history locally alive.

What local history had in those days was stuff. Much of it was inadequately housed, not all of it was cataloged, but it was preserved and was considered treasure. Those were the days of lantern slides, of rows of exhibit cases containing arrowheads and other items lined up one by one, and of talks read from long handwritten pages. I do know what I am talking about because I knew those places well. I began doing local history in that antediluvian era, and I loved it. But the winds of change were blowing, and I loved that too, even more.

We all know the pitfalls of dating a trend to a precise time, and though I contend that things began to change in 1976 when the United States celebrated its Bicentennial, the roots of and reasons for that change are embedded in earlier times. By 1976 a variety of trends, people, interests, and concerns came together to effect a change in local history, creating a vibrant new field of inquiry.

Of great importance is that, by the 1960s, the academic profession was itself giving birth to new forms and interests, discovering new documents and asking interesting questions of older materials. The origins of this can be found with the activities of the Annales School in France. Beginning in the late 1920s, a number of French historians looked beyond military, political, ecclesiastical, and diplomatic events to consider social and economic forces on people and on times. These historians—Marc Bloch and Lucien Febvre, then Fernand Braudel in the next generation, and Emmanuel Leroy Ladurie in the next—stressed the need to see *histoire totale*—or a history explored by using a variety of sources and historical techniques over time and generally place specific. This history made its way into the world of American scholarship following World War II.

Also in the world of scholarship, there was the twentieth-century development of the field of urban history, reflecting that, as historian Richard Hofstadter has commented, "The United States was born in the country and has moved to the city."[2] Historians noting this demographic shift began asking questions about population concentration, industrialization, function, and the development of community culture and society in America's urban places. Urban history was greatly informed by sociology and issues current in U.S. city life, beginning with strife and developing into discussions of renewal. In the decades since 1933, when Arthur M. Schlesinger Sr. published *The Rise of the City, 1878–1898,*[3] the field has grown exponentially.

In England, George Hoskins (1908–1992) and H. P. R. Finberg (1900–1974), who established the Department of English Local History at Leicester University, defined local history in that country. English demographic historians created the Cambridge Group in 1964 to study household and family composition by using census and tax lists, baptismal records, and other statistical information by, at first, using punch cards (and the folklore suggests using knitting needles to sort them!) and then moving onto computer spreadsheets. Their methods and questions caused a stir in American academic circles, as did the books of English historian E. P. Thompson (1924–1993).[4]

In addition, by the 1960s there was well in place among American historians something called the "new social history," which drew from and expanded on all these historical influences. In the 1970s, graduate students moved from campus to community in search of hitherto ignored documents and new lines of inquiry. The new social history opened exciting areas of investigation, expanding the cast of characters whose histories might be examined and advocating new source materials and new methods.

This activity among academic historians had implications for local history as scholars appeared in local archives, looked at local sources, and used them rather differently than before. The questions asked by the academy, however, were soon being considered on the local level. An example of this change might be documented in the field of women's history. There were women in historical societies, of course, and most local archives contained materials created by or about women, though much of this information had been considered of little value. The publication in 1971 of the first three volumes of *Notable American Women* sent local historians in search of the notable women of their own places. This energy soon spread to investigations of ethnicity and race as the cast of characters of interest to local historians expanded.

What the academic historians were doing was only one influence on the local scene, for the academic historians, as well as those in localities, were exploring topics that were also part of the national political agenda in that era of America's second war on itself—the era of civil rights and antiwar protest. The rise of black power, women's rights, ethnicity, and the American Indian Movement can be seen reflected in the questions historians asked and gave rise to, eventually, historical trends that dominated the last quarter of the twentieth century.

The preservation movement must also be credited with stimulating an interest in and a use for local history. Although preservation activities could be found in the nineteenth century, the National Trust for Historic Preservation became potent in the 1960s, especially after the passage of the National Historic Preservation Act of 1966, which energized preservation activity all over the country. The focus moved from Mount Vernon—and other similar special places—to Main Street. The preservationists had to become activists to persuade communities of the value of identifying and maintaining our architectural heritage, and in fighting those battles they needed to delve into the records to document threatened structures. This brought a great deal of new energy and a bevy of active people into the historical archive. Although local history and preservation might have become partners working from one base, in most cases the local historians were uncomfortable with the confrontational tactics of the preservationists and the preservationists were impatient with the stodgy, careful approach taken by those in historical societies. Generally, in many places two organizations evolved. What the preservationists achieved was a visibility for the architectural remains of the past, reclaimed and then put back into use. They focused on the use of local documents and local information, clearly articulated for the community. They were, in the long run, very good for our communities and for local history.

Along with preservation, the 1960s experienced Foxfire, an innovative teaching technique that sent children into neighborhoods to uncover and preserve folkways that had carried over from the past. Foxfire spread from Georgia, where it began in Raban Gap, to schools around the country. It coincided with an expansion of academic interest in folklore and a general interest in the handmade and traditional crafts. By 1975 the concept of "Small Is Beautiful" focused on life outside large urban centers just as some Americans began to investigate what was called an "alternative lifestyle."[5]

Other things worked to promote the local. History Day began in 1974 and challenged students to create local history projects. Many of these projects were stunning in their use of local sources and especially of their presentations at local history fairs and competitions. The National Endowments, chartered in 1965, received greater funding and directives to become more responsive to localities. By the mid-1970s they had spawned state arts and humanities councils with funding distributed statewide by decentralized programs. This challenged and improved local history because, to get grants, the standards set by the councils had to be met. For the first time, in many cases, organizations regularized boards of directors, terms of appointment, and training. To be competitive, history projects of all sorts had to be carefully thought through, and experts needed to be consulted and hired. For local history to be competitive, it had to become responsible and professional. All of this was good for the independent scholar and historical agency alike. During that era, the Newberry Library of Chicago sponsored a series of Local and Family History Seminars that stressed historical techniques, including quantitative skills and a familiarity with computer use—then something of a surprise to historians, now indispensable.

In 1976 the public history program at the University of California at Santa Barbara ushered in a new era by preparing students for careers in state and county historical societies and in government and industrial archives. In addition, beginning in 1979, *Cobblestone Magazine* brought lively and topical historical issues to children. Regional programs also appeared: the Appalachian Studies Center, the Long Island Studies Association, the Center for Great Plains Studies, and the Center for the Study of Southern Culture. All of these developments, and others, fostered a sense of the importance of the local.

On bookshelves there were new books of local history, while older, standard histories were reprinted or indexed. Historical societies, many to this point static, saw that they had something important to offer their communities. Community colleges began listing courses in local history; and in many states local history offerings in the public schools were relocated into the elementary grades, where those teaching them were challenged to improve the quality of their lessons, thereby producing a new emphasis on Native Americans, on ethnic groups in the community, and sometimes on women of note.

All of this was going on at the same time that this country celebrated the bicentennial of the American Revolution. By 1976, despite national commissions and programs, many people realized that the only meaningful celebrations of the nation's independence would be those in America's localities. Local committees were formed, celebrations were planned, and except for the appearance of the tall ships on national television, most of the memorable aspects of the bicentennial occurred at home.

Most significant during this vibrant quarter century was the impact of the publication in 1976–1977 of *Roots* and its broadcast as a television series. Alex Haley's story of Kunta Kinte, his abduction from his African home, his days of slavery, and his family thereafter riveted viewers and spawned an interest in genealogy among people of varying backgrounds, many of whom had not before thought their family history might be interesting or even traceable. The abiding importance of *Roots* is not in Haley's dramatized genealogy, although that stirred emotions in a great number of people, it is rather in its showing that African Americans were able to put names and places on their ancestry. This propelled others into the field; people who might have thought that their ancestries were impossible to track, or were too recent or insignificant to locate, became interested in their own backgrounds. Suddenly, the microfilm room in the National Archives, long the haunt of genealogists seeking family connections for admission to elite organizations, became the haunt of young and elderly, black and white, of those whose families had come to this country during the twentieth century as well as those who had arrived on the *Mayflower*. The second stunning shift in genealogical interest, of course, occurred in the 1990s with widespread computer use and the links made possible by the Internet. Today it is estimated that millions of people all over the country are involved in researching aspects of their family histories and television programs promoting the identification of ancestors proliferate like a batch of cousins.

Over the past quarter century history has blossomed. Television featured Charles Kuralt's programs about localities and local personalities, *American Experience* brought history stories to public television, and the History Channel appeared and proved to be popular. For Americans, participation has always been more attractive than simply being part of an audience, and while children played with G.I. Joe and Barbie, many adults threw themselves into Revolutionary and Civil War battle reenactments, complete with careful attention paid to uniforms, equipment, and troop organizations replicating those of the original battlefield.[6] In 1990, Ken Burns gave us *The Civil War* on public television, followed by other programs giving voices and often images of participants, another reinforcement of the importance of local documents and participants in notable events.

Tourism flourished too. Our national parks were visited by greater numbers than ever before. Taking notice of changing historical fashions, the National Park Service embarked on a bold program of revising exhibits to reflect new historical trends and developed new sites. There was the Lowell, Massachusetts, mill that became the first industrial National Historic Site, authorized in 1978. There was the Maggie Walker House in Richmond, Virginia, celebrating the life of a woman from a humble background who pioneered in hair-care products for African Americans. Eventually, in the late 1990s, the concept came into being of a noncontiguous park to commemorate the many places and people important to the abolition movement and the Underground Railroad. In addition, the exhibits and labels at national park sites underwent a transformation, stressing inclusivity of gender, race, and ethnicity and the situational problems of events. There was, in addition, a blossoming of new and smaller museums and historical societies, sometimes fostered by the need to preserve a building, often spurred by the belief that state and county historical associations were not interested in the really local story. These were places where the professionalization of local history was eschewed in favor of local hands-on control and direction.

There were historical controversies, too, during the past quarter century— sometimes small affairs, sometimes large—that erupted into the public sphere. It suddenly seemed as if things historical mattered and were worth arguing about in public. There was loud discussion during the planning stages for the 1992 Columbian Celebration. In that case, questions were raised about the intent and meaning of the celebration, about whose history was being celebrated, and about the fact that the "discovery" of the New World involved not a lost or empty continent as was often portrayed, but, rather, a place already occupied by native peoples with vibrant cultures. The old verbal jousting between Scandinavians and Italians over who had arrived first on North American shores faded completely in the face of the new controversy.

History mattered when the Civil War battlefield at Manassas, Virginia, was threatened by development. In 1921, the Sons of Confederate Veterans had established a park on the site. In 1940, the federal government became steward of the land and created Manassas National Battlefield Park. From that time forward, the site was dogged by problems, culminating in 1993 when the Walt Disney Company announced plans to construct a theme park just northwest of the battlefield. Alerted by the media and the National Trust for Historic Preservation, historians came forward to defend the importance of safeguarding the park, and the controversy was played out in the press. Positions hardened: a Senate hearing was held, battle lines drawn, and, in 1994, Disney withdrew.[7]

There was also controversy about the renaming of the site of George Custer's 1876 battle. The history of that name is actually interesting and telling. In 1879, the secretary of war established the site as a national cemetery to protect the graves. Then, in 1886, it was designated the National Cemetery of Custer's Battlefield in order to include burials from other battles, and in 1926 it was appended to it the Reno-Benteen Battlefield. In 1940, the site was transferred from the War Department, and in 1946, it was redesignated as Custer Battlefield National Monument. In 1991, the National Park Service renamed the site the Little Bighorn Battlefield National Monument, reflecting the fact that there had been two sides involved in the battle—two very different points of view.[8]

History mattered again when historians at the Smithsonian Institution's National Air and Space Museum, on the Mall in Washington, D.C., set out to examine the use of the atomic bomb against Japan in August 1945. There were, Tom Engelhardt and Edward Linenthal have noted, "two stories—of a weapon that brought peace and victory, and of a weapon that brought destruction and fear to the world."[9] Objects to be displayed included the fuselage of the *Enola Gay*, the B-29 from which the bomb was dropped on Hiroshima on August 6. The controversy was taken up by more sides than there are on a polygon: there were the historians who did not want to sugarcoat the past and for whom new material provided new insight; there were historians who believed that the scripts for the exhibit needed to be tempered; there were the veterans who had been in the armed forces in 1945 who were saved from death because the war was finally brought to an end; there were the American Legion and those with a military point of view; there were the advocates of World War II as the "good war" and those who were against all wars; there was Congress, in addition, from which significant funding for the Smithsonian came; and there was also the museum administration, muffled by the storm that broke all around it. In the end, and even after two exhibit scripts were written, the exhibit that was finally mounted in 1995, featuring and enshrining the *Enola Gay*, but "drastically scaled back." The controversy, which was played out in the media with many participants, was about the difference among "facts" and memory and careful historical consideration.

History also mattered when the United States Holocaust Memorial Museum was chartered by Congress in 1980. The museum is dedicated to a subject that many people thought could never be displayed. Yet the museum curators innovated in concept and design, personalizing the horror of that era by giving faces to the victims. The museum staff also innovated with a startling website. The debunkers claimed that the Holocaust never happened; they placed disturbing advertisements in a number of newspapers, especially those on college campuses, raising the added issue of the ethical use of the press. Those whose lives and families had been directly touched by the horror of the Nazi past were affronted by the charges and testified to their pain and loss. Over these issues, there was loud debate joined by many voices, and history mattered.

There was, too, what came to be called "the History Wars," waged over a number of issues but calling into question how history was being taught in the public schools, what should be taught, what sort of accountability public-school teachers had to the taxpaying public, and the nature of history projects funded by the National Endowments. Central to the battle were the National History Standards, which had been developed by the National Center for History in the Schools at the University of California at Los Angeles with money from the National Endowment for the Humanities (NEH). The battle erupted in 1994 when Lynne Cheney, who headed NEH at the time the grant was awarded, turned against the standards even before they were made public. The problem, as Cheney saw it, was that the standards were "anti-Western, anti–Dead White Male, anti–free enterprise," and politically correct. History had democratized; it had become inclusive, aware of nondominant cultures and events, and in doing so it brought down the wrath of those invested in traditional historical topics and method. History, in this instance, certainly mattered.[10]

Yet with interest in history at a peak, investigators discovered that historical knowledge among Americans was weak. So even as Americans visited historical museums in greater numbers, books of popular history sold, people joined historical societies and reenactment groups, the American Girl dolls from different historic periods sold well and were collected by those who could afford them, and genealogical fever spread, our knowledge of history appeared to be dismal.

What became popular during this era was heritage. We protected our heritage, we studied our heritage, and we exploited it. Companies offered "heritage" homes, "heritage" tours, and "heritage" dishes. We overdosed on the word, which came to mean, in the end, very little. So little did "heritage" mean that it was used interchangeably with the word "history." People who collected family photographs, and others who were interested in reenactments, were said to be "steeped in our national heritage." These activities, however, were more likely to have been undertaken out of a personal interest in family or in battle uniforms, and battles themselves, rather than in learning and understanding as a historian would. Being interested in history, which is, of course, a good thing, is not the same as knowing or understanding history. Americans, when tested, were shown to be ignorant of our national past; calling an interest in one's heritage history does not make it so. Historian David Lowenthal writes, "Heritage is not history, even when it mimics history. It uses historical traces and tells historical tales, but these tales and traces are stitched into fables that are open neither to critical analysis nor to comparative scrutiny." Historical knowledge looks at the past in order to understand it, whereas the heritage industry was interested mainly in exploiting it.[11]

During this era, history and historical sites became destinations. As our communities changed from places that produced goods and products to places that could no longer identify themselves as manufacturing or commercial centers, those in charge of tourism noticed that history sites could draw tourism dollars. Communities all over the country began to market their local histories, along with their festivals, natural scenery, sporting events, and museums, hoping to lure the casual tourist, the senior-citizen bus tour, the convention, or the family out in the car for the day or a week exploring the countryside. Thus dawned the age of cultural tourism, usually promoted by tourism experts, by tourist bureaus in chambers of commerce, or from a city or state tourism department.

How could all this not have an effect upon local history? Debates about history, the use of history, and the need for historical sites and an appreciation of those in a community; an emphasis on the local, the homemade, and the hometown as well as a search for rootedness in a bare-root world, led individuals and communities to the historical society archive, to talks about the local, to an interest in preserving the local, and to questions about how this or that came about. That there was money—some money, not a lot— gave direction to the programming of historical associations and brought many of those organizations into a new era. That there was a need for scholarship led new people into the local archive where new questions were asked and in some places an alliance was forged between the academy and America's localities. There was genuine interest in the local.

After years of historical societies scrimping to get by—and doing so with a minimum of community enthusiasm—historical societies, historic houses, and museums of all sorts began to turn up the lights and redesign and improve the captions on exhibits. This transformation was overseen, in many cases, by trained young people coming out of history departments and public history and museum programs. These were young professionals who were accustomed by training to think about history in new and exciting ways.

They brought with them current historical trends, including an interest in race, class, and ethnicity; in women; in institutions such as asylums, the distribution of charity, and the disposal of garbage; in the development of local government and of markets; and in the relationship of the local to the regional and national.

Historical associations basked in this new attention, but they also learned the value of cooperation. History museums joined with other cultural institutions to promote the various opportunities for tourism in a community. This step has been fostered by the tourism industry and by the money that is sometimes available from state and local tourism grants. In a sense, local societies joined the communities they document, and being out in the streets, at meetings, and public gatherings, has given them and local history a greater presence. People came to value what local history has to offer.

Local history also appeared in a variety of guises. Sometimes it is found in newspapers in the form of history columns, in objects of local history exhibited in courthouse or banks, as photographs that appear on buses, in programs on local access television, or on regional public radio and television stations. Local history can be "heard from" when environmental impact statements are created for the development of parcels of land, when a building is threatened, or when a celebration is to be held. Local history participates in community life with the result that community members expect it to be there—and this is a change.

AND WHAT OF TOMORROW?

The important question is not what was created over the final quarter century of the twentieth century but, rather, how local history was to maintain this popularity. How would local history and interest in things local continue to be popular, useful, and well-enough funded to do a good job? How might local history be aided from fading back into the more shadowy position it found itself in after the turn of the twentieth century, after the excitement of the Centennial faded and new realities took hold? How would local history fare in the twenty-first century?

Local history, meaning all those individuals, organizations, buildings, resources, and uses that have been found for it, needed to continue to function as a community educator. In addition to producing good books and pamphlets and intelligent exhibits and lectures, this meant seeing and responding to community needs, being part of the local landscape rather than sitting apart from it, and cooperating with other cultural institutions and with public officials. It meant that local history needed to understand the modern, living community it served, not just the descendants of those buried in the local cemetery.

This also meant not just informing people about the facts of what happened in their hometowns but actually finding ways to develop an understanding of the way in which history grows and evolves—a historical consciousness. This is not the same as giving an answer to a history question, but rather it is all about showing how the history of a place came about: the local influences and those from outside—national and international. It meant and means today looking at trends over time. It means, most of all, not treating the past like a golden era to be emulated and admired but, instead, treating it as simply the past. Community education, I think, should show how the locality created its own palimpsest, each unique piece related to others that come after, not necessarily leading forward directly but in a more haphazard fashion, merging from one era to another, each reflecting some of the universal, some of the homegrown, some of what came before. We need to remember all the various segments of the community that are in our charge, including not only the standard suspects but also local and county legislators, representatives of the media, and even historical-organization board members who should be subjected to historical knowledge along with an understanding of the current budget.

The key to this, I am sure, is inclusion. That means inclusion in collection interests, exhibits, and lecture topics. It means investigating the history of a wide variety of people and situations rather than only the healthy, wealthy, and wise. It means opening the doors of historical societies to poets and musicians, making alliances with preservationists and others interested in place, answering the questions of local legislators even before they have the questions formed, and inviting groups into the historical society that have not been there before. It means looking at the outlying areas and helping them have a presence. The trend of proliferation of smaller and smaller historical groups weakens some central organizations and also dilutes the energy and financial underpinnings needed to keep one good society growing but those newly minted museums, historic houses, and historical organizations cannot be ignored. When smaller associations spring up, as they have all over the country, hands need to be extended to aid them in their efforts.

Robert Archibald, in his interesting memoir of his life in local history, talks about this need for inclusion and his experiences with broadening the base for the Missouri Historical Society. Reading his book *A Place to Remember: Using History to Build Community*, especially chapters 6 and 7, should be required for all historical society directors and their boards. [12]

I have been struck by the enthusiasm with which people undertake genealogical research, generally adhering to high standards of accountability and thoroughness in their searches. I might quibble about the limited questions asked, but I am always impressed at the energy put to the task and at the amount of money genealogists devote to their quests. There is energy, too, among those who become active preservationists. People don painter's pants and wield scrapers. Watching them become involved, become so intimately concerned, has made me realize that this same sort of energy and personal involvement could be and should be harnessed for the benefit of local history. We need to find ways of involving people beyond paying dues, visiting an exhibit, or buying a book. We need to extend to the local history audience the same privilege of participating in an active way that is natural in these other pursuits. We tend to keep all the "fun" of doing history to ourselves and then deliver the results to the public. Sharing the research and planning and communicating about local history with others would be consistent with our role as public educators.

There are strategies that might be employed. Appointing a local history photography squad might be one for those adept with cameras—a category of people who seem to be everywhere these days. These folks could document the contemporary community, its festivals, its rituals, and its demolitions and natural disasters, as well as aspects of ordinary life. Photo squads could discuss what represents the community today, think of ways to bring community rituals to a broader audience, and create important documents for the present and the future. They should also be totally involved with the process of documentation—that of preservation, identification, and display of their contributions.

Those involved with local history might sponsor or encourage groups devoted to writing life histories or writing about contemporary life in a town. It is our job to show others how their work fosters knowledge of contemporary local history and to help them collect or copy their observations. We need to show people how the artifacts of the past talk to us today, how the documents of everyday life illuminate an era or an episode. These folks should have the satisfaction of contributing to the local archive, to local knowledge.

In 1988, we documented one day in my county. People were invited to write a diary account, tell the story of a neighbor's life or contribution to the community, describe the mall or main street, discuss teen slang, and tell local stories. We received more than six thousand entries in a variety of forms: diary entries, reports, essays, poems, videos, drawings. When this same exercise was copied in the state of Utah, there were in excess of five hundred thousand entries. A number of other communities around the country have used variations on this theme, garnering priceless commentary about their places and also involving citizens in the process of creating history and knowing that it would be valued. This is a gift to the future.[13]

In 2013, we celebrated the twenty-fifth anniversary of One Day in Ithaca by inviting folks to consider life now. Again the response was stunning. A number of people who had written twenty-five years ago wrote again, mostly about change over time. They told us what had happened in the past quarter century to themselves and to the community as they viewed it. They talked about loss, growth, retirement, coping with the weather, and things that concerned them. Surprisingly, a whole new crop of people talked about their decision to remain here, even when jobs or family called them elsewhere. Some wrote about going elsewhere and then returning, and a number of folks who had gone away discussed their memories of growing up here. One young boy recalled a vivid memory of lying on the lawn watching cars stream into and out of the city. He remembered observing that most of the automobiles leaving were large vehicles while those entering were predominantly VW Beetles. I was astonished by his recall and his observation, especially so, when I realized that it was my son telling me something about his childhood I had never known.

In 1988, we published a book of entries. This time we are considering more modern ways—including a CD and a website—on which to display these comments. Some people still want a book and that is under consideration. Times change and how we "deliver" local history has the ability to take on new and exciting forms.

Adult local-history workshops, as I discuss in the coda to chapter 6, are also valuable. They result in solid information about the given topic and a group of people who have undergone training—sometimes a formal process with an instructor, often by thinking through the project by themselves to give their work structure. Some groups remain together after completion to take on other topics; other groups function for one project and then disband.

The benefit of all these exercises is that what people contribute is shown to be useful and important, and in the process of working as photographers or local history researchers, people share their knowledge, learn about the sources available, and contribute to what is known about a place. Equally important is that those who participate learn about the nature of history—its shiftiness, its elusiveness, and its joys—and they grow in their understanding of place.

Local history has had remarkable visibility over the past quarter century. It has been nourished, expanded, and extended beyond a small group or a club-like setting; it is seen to be useful, and it helps define the community. It is up to us to see that this continues, not to keep ourselves in business but because the places where we live benefit when we and others engage in doing local history.

NOTES

1. Howard Mansfield, *In the Memory House* (Golden, CO: Fulcrum Publishing, 1993), 270.
2. Richard Hofstadter, *The Age of Reform*, p. 23 (1960).
3. Arthur M. Schlesinger Sr., *The Rise of the City, 1878–1898* (New York: Macmillan, 1933).

4. See the entries for English Local History in the *Encyclopedia of Local History* (Lanham, MD: AltaMira Press, 2012).

5. Elliot Wigginton created Foxfire when he taught in Raban Gap, Georgia, where he instructed his students to study the activities of people who were engaged in old crafts. The idea spread from there and was adapted by schoolteachers everywhere. The first Foxfire book appeared in 1961 from Raban Gap; after that there were at least eight books in the series, most of the later ones issued by various New York publishers. See John L. Puckett, *Foxfire Reconsidered: A Twenty-Year Experiment in Progressive Education* (Urbana: University of Illinois Press, 1989). See also E. F. Schumacher, *Small Is Beautiful: Economics as If People Mattered* (New York: Harper and Row, 1975).

6. See Tony Horwitz, *Confederates in the Attic: Dispatches from the Unfinished Civil War* (New York: Vintage, 1999).

7. See Joan M. Zenzen, *Battling for Manassas: The Fifty-Year Preservation Struggle at Manassas National Battlefield Park* (University Park: Pennsylvania State University Press, 1998).

8. 6. The information about this site is from the Office of Public Affairs, The National Parks: Index 2001–2003 (Washington, DC: US Department of the Interior, n.d.). See also www.nps.gov.

9. See Edward T. Linenthal and Tom Engelhardt, eds., *History Wars: The* Enola Gay *and Other Battles for the American Past* (New York: Henry Holt and Co., 1996), 2. See also Martin Harwit, *An Exhibit Denied: Lobbying the History of* Enola Gay (New York: Copernicus Press, 1996).

10. See Gary B. Nash, Charlotte Crabtree, and Ross E. Dunn, *History on Trial: Culture Wars and the Teaching of the Past* (New York: Knopf, 1997). The quote is from a review of the book by Michael Bérubé, "Our Children Deserve to Know," *The Nation*, December 22, 1997.

11. David Lowenthal, *The Past Is a Foreign Country* (New York: Cambridge University Press, 1985); Michael Kammen, "History Is Our Heritage: The Past in Contemporary American Culture," in *Historical Literacy: The Case for History in American Education*, ed. Paul Gagnon and the Bradley Commission on History in Schools (New York: Macmillan, 1989).

12. Robert Archibald, *A Place to Remember: Using History to Build Community* (Walnut Creek, CA: AltaMira Press, 1999).

13. See Carol Kammen, ed., *One Day in Ithaca: May 17, 1988* (Ithaca: Ithaca Centennial Commission, 1989); and Shannon R. Hoskins, ed., *Faces of Utah: A Portrait* (Salt Lake City: Gibbs-Smith Publisher, 1996).

Coda to Chapter 9

One Last Thing

I would like to return to Marc Bloch's observation that to be a good historian one must know the present as well as investigate the past. Without knowledge and interest in what is going on in our communities today, without some understanding of human nature, Bloch warns that we will be only antiquarians. This is a wise caution and one I take to heart. I would add that because local historians are keen observers of the past of place, they might also use their historical skills to record and write about the present. Who better to turn an eye on a community to see what there is today? What better legacy to leave the future than a series of observations of our own time?

Before panic or rebellion sets in, I should explain that I do not mean abandoning historical research. Nor do I intend this to be regarded as a finished product. Rather, I like to think of our observations as a way of giving real space to thoughts about the places in which we live that will carry over to another time some of the flavor and texture of our own era. There are a variety of formats that could be considered: observations might be a series of paragraphs in a notebook or on a computer, short essays kept in a drawer, photographs with extensive annotations, scrapbooks, or poems. What I am not suggesting is a diary or even a journal chronicling one's personal journey through life: that is another thing altogether. Rather, I am thinking of William Lambarde's *Perambulations of Kent* in which he noted what he saw—although his book chronicled one journey and what I have in mind is more of an ongoing commentary: short pieces about what is observed, paragraphs about the places in which we live.

These short essays would be general and specific at the same time. They would be personal observations, meaning they would reflect one view, sometimes bolstered with information from experts, such as the police for the number of arrests per month, the SPCA for the number of animals shelter at the time, the school board for the number of pupils enrolled in the local school, or the number of bus routes and riders that serve the district. The election clerk could provide figures about the local turnout for municipal elections, with additional information from the newspaper about local issues. The goal would be for the local historian to identify things about a community that are important to that place, significant markers of change that has already taken place or is occurring, or what it is like to live in a particular spot. These could be topics that a historical society director might assign a board of trustees to bring to each meeting or topics taken on by senior-citizen writing groups or by youngsters in school; others can certainly be involved, but my interest is to have local historians think in terms of contemporary documentation.

For some people, this addition to the local historian's duties might cause discomfort, in which case the suggestion can be easily ignored. I will not show up at your doorstep and demand your notebook, nor will I send Federal Express to collect commentary from you. For other people, this sort of informal observation might feel unnatural because it depends not upon sources from the archive but on evidence of a different sort.

This type of writing is more personal; it depends entirely on the interests and abilities of each individual; it is empirical. And for the most part these comments will have a different texture from the documents already in our archives because they are a planned exercise and not the sort of notations found in a diary, for example, where the author has written what was probably thought to be a private observation, not one that started out to be more objective and public; or in letters, when one knows the recipient; or in other sources of a familiar type.

Since hoping for this sort of new material to come into the archives—for the sake of the writers who will become more aware of their lives in history and for future historians—all this has come about in the form of blogs. People *are* writing. Many people are commenting on their lives, their concerns, their hopes: they are sending out from their various devices messages all day long. This is a very exciting new phenomenon, for the electronic world allows greater communication over space. Our circles widen and broaden; we meet others in the ether and discover similarities and common concerns. There is an ease and naturalness in a blog post and most that I have read are to the point and interesting. I learn things from blogs, I feel connected to what is going on even without leaving my study. This is exciting and makes me want to create a blog. Who will be at the other end? I have no idea but I suspect they (assuming that there might be more than one) will make themselves known and will add to my solitary commentary. We will make and remake communities, share interests, and feel, perhaps, not so alone in our concerns. I follow the blog messages that Bill Hosley sends me from Connecticut, those from Peter Feinman and Bruce Dearstyne whose interests are similar to mine, from New York—whose interests are mine. I get images and maps on a regular basis from Bill Hecht in Union Springs, a small community north of my home on the lake. I follow Linda Norris and I used to get Nina Simon but somewhere the connection was severed. I follow Simon St. Laurent's "Living in Dryden," a blog that captures information in the press and notices about events going on in that small New York town. Just recently I began reading the posts of Marjory O'Toole writing from Little Compton, Rhode Island, and if I am not reading further, it is because I don't know about others. What a lovely world this has become.

Giving a talk in Cheyenne, Wyoming, a few years ago, I commented to the historians and archivists present that in order to learn about Cheyenne I had looked at the blogs about that city and found that the most active group blogging seemed to be the gay community, who developed a lively fellowship online. The problem that I see is that these electronic postings exist in such an ethereal form that they are not yet useful to historians unless they give permission for their posts to be collected and downloaded. I know that this involves legal questions and also technical ones that I am not competent to answer, but I also know that there is great material floating about in the air above us, telling us about who they are and who we are and we need to find ways of capturing it just as we collected all those little black diaries from the nineteenth century.

Wouldn't it be interesting if we could catch some local bloggers' attention now and then to suggest a topic they might tackle? We might ask about local elections, the plans for new sidewalks, the recent festival (since we seem to have given up parades).

What topic? Not to ignore all the standard topics that local history has touched upon, there are topics less frequently tackled.

- community causes; festivals that mark the year; divergences of opinion; places to be in touch with nature and what they mean
- local signs of the change of seasons; changes on Main Street; changes in occupation, ethnicity
- dangerous local places: natural and created
- things that change the skyline
- where you can glimpse the past: the uncluttered view
- the many communities to which you belong: geographic, ethnic, occupational, affectional or voluntary, extended family, linguistic
- sound history; what you hear throughout the day and also what sounds you remember from the past
- the local palate of odors: smells that evoke things today and those that make you think of the past

- remnants of our agricultural past: in some places this might be turned around to think about the small commercial centers that once were but no longer are
- routines of place: rush hours, quiet times
- meeting places: these will differ by age, occupation, and other factors (I am thinking here of teens in a mall, ladies at lunch, people meeting at civic groups, in churches, and so on)
- use of the land and how we think about places in the community: used land; unused land; fallow land; misused places
- neutral places in a community: the library, perhaps
- community institutions: banks, groceries, meeting halls, concert halls, people who are institutions
- traffic patterns: where the local bottlenecks are, what places to avoid at particular hours; how to get places and where those places where people's lives intersect (the mall?); shifts in shopping patterns
- crime
- volunteer roles
- generations: the elderly: what they are doing today; infant care: who is doing it; those out of sight: who is not seen; who is now visible (I am thinking of the physically handicapped and how we have made places more accessible); the family: how it is organized today; women's roles; what children do; special changes within a home: what sorts of spaces are valued most; what do real estate ads tell us
- entertainment; home entertainment and how that has changed (are there still bridge clubs or are those groups now all book clubs); shared entertainments and the places they happen; special festive times

The topics are endless but sadly, time is not. We need to choose our interests and then pursue them as best we can. Local history provides us with a platform on which we can showcase our interests, a community's quirks, and a region's patterns, and where we can focus in many ways on local documents of many sorts. Local history is actually all around and underfoot just waiting for us to pay it attention. It is a pursuit where we can find infinite delight in knowing about place, in examining human nature, and especially in exploring ourselves in and over time.

Index

Washington State Historical Society, 79
water-cure hospital, 103
Westchester County Historical Society, 132
Wharton Esherick Museum, 75
White, Gilbert, 45, 117
White, Grace Miller, 103
White League, 27
Whitman, Marcus, 128
Whitman, Narcissa, 128, 131
Wigginton, Elliot, 164n5
wills, 96
Wilson, Amy H., 101
Wisner, William, 83, 84, 88
women, 28, 29, 35, 103, 153; abortion and, 48; cooking and, 56; as patrician historians, 13–14; recipes and, 55
Women's Rights Convention, 114
Women's Rights National Historic Park, 114
workshops, 140, 148–149, 163
World War I, 14

World War II, 47, 53, 77, 131; *Enola Gay* and, 36, 157; public schools and, 17
writing, 2–4, 166; boosterism and, 4; commemorative, 3; as competition, 4; of congregational history, 86–91; culture and, 3; as oral presentation, 4; patrician historians and, 2; patterns of, 2
Writing Local History Today: A Guide to Researching, Publishing, and Marketing Your Book (Mason and Calder), 102
Written in Stone: Public Monuments in Changing Societies (Levinson), 27
W. W. Munsell and Company, 12

Xenophon, 6

Yale University, 114
youth, 4, 5; labor and, 60

Zeldin, Theodore, 136
Zero Dark Thirty (film), 73
Zonabend, Françoise, 21, 50

About the Author

Carol Kammen has been writing about doing local history for many years. The first edition of this book came out in 1985; this edition is greatly pruned and expanded. She has edited *The Encyclopedia of Local History* (two editions) for AltaMira Press and AASLH and has written editorials for *History News* since 1995. In addition she has written a history of her county, of the city in which she lives, and *Cornell: Glorious to View* (2003) and *Part and Apart: The African American Experience at Cornell, 1865–1945* (2008) and edited *First Person Cornell: Students' Letters, Diaries, Email and Blogs* (2006). She has also written two dozen dramatic presentations using local history, including *Between the Lines, Peaches and Bird, The Language of War*, and others, and writes a history column for her local newspaper. She lives in Ithaca, New York, taught for many years at Cornell University, and serves as the Tompkins County Historian.